Everlasting Prophetic

Bridging Heaven to Earth

Annie Blouin

Life Press Publishing

Published by Life Press Publishing

Wake Forest, NC 27587

Printed in the United States of America

ISBN 978-0-9978847-0-8

Religion / Christian Life / Spiritual Growth

$25.00

Also by Annie Blouin

Everlasting Doors:

When the Supernatural Penetrates American Politics

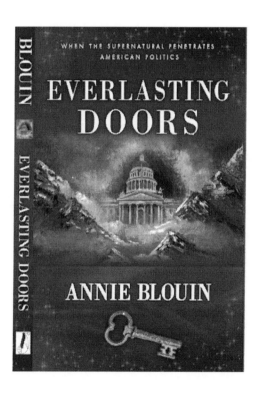

Dedication

This book is dedicated to my daughter, Grace Ann. Her heart for the Lord and for people is pure and lovely. I love you, Sweetheart.

Acknowledgements

As with any project, writing a book requires a team effort. I'd like to thank my husband, Joe for his unwavering love and support and for always championing me. I love you for always and forever.

Thanks to Father God for His unconditional love. You're worth it all.

Thanks to my children, Madeleine, Grace and Joey for being patient while I finished this project. I love you guys and am enjoying watching you run your races well with Jesus.

Thanks to CTF Raleigh, a wonderful church family and CTF School of Revival for running passionately after a good Father. Special thanks to Duncan & Kate Smith, Murray & Ash Smith, Aaron & Jacquelyn Mitchell. I love all of you and am thankful for you.

Thanks to Bill Johnson, Kris Vallotton, and Team from Bethel Church Redding. Your hearts for worshipping Jesus and pursuing Heaven on Earth has impacted our family and our generations immeasurably. Thanks for all you've pioneered.

Thanks to Suzanne, Amanda, Holly and Christy and all the lovely ladies and gentlemen of the Redding prophetic group for your hearts to pursue God and the prophetic. Your willingness and passion to explore the prophetic realm together continue to inspire me.

Thanks to Margaret Cantrell for your professional editing and for your friendship. I'm thankful for you!

Contents

INTRODUCTION

I fell deeply in love with the Father, Son and Holy Spirit when I was baptized in the Holy Spirit October 6, 2002. I had gotten saved April 13, 1997 when I witnessed the love and power of the Lord but my heart fully awakened in 2002. If you're like me, someone who knew the Lord but didn't feel passionate for Him, ask the Holy Spirit to fill you like He did for the disciples in the Upper Room. His power and love is like a rocket booster to life. Power, purpose and passion come with the Baptism of the Holy Spirit.

My gift for seeing into the supernatural realms opened fully in 2002. It's been a wild ride!

One day during my time with the Lord, He asked me what I wanted from Him. The way He asked reminded me of how He asked Solomon what He wanted. I felt the holiness of the moment. I carefully searched my heart and considered His question. After much thought, I asked the Lord for an anointing on my life that whomever encounters me would develop a great hunger for more of Jesus.

Beloved, I pray that as you read this book, you would encounter the One who loves you beyond measure and hunger for deep intimacy with Him.

Annie Blouin

CHAPTER 1

WHY THE PROPHETIC

The Creator created by speaking the world into existence. The Word made flesh came and dwelt among us. Jesus, the King of kings and Lord of lords is still speaking to us and we have the privilege of Him speaking through us. The Prophetic: The language of Heaven released through people, events and nature. We have the awesome ability to cause men to see themselves for whom they are and watch as they rise up to worship the Lord, in turn. The Prophetic: Kisses from a magnificent Father. The Prophetic: Intimacy with a good Daddy. The Prophetic: Power to Disciple Nations. You and I have been commissioned to release the world into an encounter with Destiny. Romans 3:23 says, "for all have sinned and fall short of the glory of God". When we prophesy people's true identity to them, they become aware of the greatness they were designed to carry, to bring God glory. Three things result: they worship God for His kindness leading to repentance and they seek Him and their destiny.

The Prophetic answers all three of peoples' heart's cries: 1. Who is God? It's the revelation of the true nature of God. 2. Who am I? True identity is revealed. 3. What am I called to do? True purpose discovered. 1 Corinthians 14:24-25 "But if all prophesy, and an unbeliever or an uninformed person comes in, he is convinced by all, he is convicted by all. And thus the secrets of his heart are revealed; and so, falling down on his face, he will worship God and report that God is truly among you."

PRAYER ACTIVATION

Spend some time with the Lord asking Him to reveal the answers to your personal heart cry. Ask Him to show you whom He is to you, who you are, and what your specific life purpose is. Be sure to journal His response. The Lord is faithful to answer these questions. However, He may take you on a journey to reveal this, so be open to His leading.

_____

_____

_____

_____

_____

_____

_____

_____

_____

_____

_____

_____

_____

The world is desperate for answers to these questions. If the Body of Christ doesn't carry the revelation through the prophetic, people turn to the occult to get answers. Fortunetellers, tarot card readers and other diviners access the spiritual realm illegally. The only true legal access is through Jesus. He is the Way, the Truth and the Life. Fallen angels, more commonly known as the demonic, give the occultist seeker answers about the past, present, and future. Most of the past and present is accurate. The future, even if positive, will encompass assignments carried out by the demonic and will always have a hidden cost.

I, unfortunately, experienced this and it's all too real. When I was in my early 20's, neither my mother nor I was a Believer. She, saddened by some family dynamics, sought out a fortuneteller. The woman "prophesied" family restoration and other things. I was very uncomfortable with what my mom had done because I sensed the evil in it. I didn't allow my mom to tell me what the woman spoke over my life. Unfortunately, not knowing didn't eliminate the consequences for my life. Soon after that event and for the next two decades, I struggled with unexplained low energy, lack of joy and health battles. I would often tell my husband that I sensed it was tied up in the spirit somehow. In the spring of 2013, I received the following prophetic word:

"I feel like you have been in a time of refinement, a refining fire time and in three weeks' time JOY will be coming home to roost in your life! Your joy, your health, your energy, your strength will return. He reminds you that His load/yoke is light. Trust in Him. He does have it all in control. Philippians 4:6 "Be anxious for nothing, but in everything by prayer and supplication, with thanksgiving, let your requests be known to God." He will bring it to pass. No worries! Hugs from your Savior!"

When I got the word, my spirit quickened to it and it confirmed to me that I was right about my joy, health, energy and strength being tied up somehow and I was encouraged about them returning in such a short amount of time. I asked God later that night about the prophetic word. He told me it was connected to my mom dying and that when she died, I would get all of that back. As He spoke, His presence filled my room with peace. Even though it was a sad transition He was telling me about, joy was in the room. I asked Him why it was connected to her. Earlier that day, she'd been confirmed to be 9 months cancer free by the Mayo Clinic and was expected to continue improving in health. The Lord told me that when she visited the fortuneteller twenty years earlier, the consequences for me were my joy, energy, strength, and health were stolen and that upon her death, the curse would be broken and I would be restored. I was simultaneously saddened by her impending death, and yet encouraged by my new life. As I was talking to the Lord, He didn't confirm or deny the 3-week timing of the prophetic word. I prepared my heart for the word to be correct. I spoke with my mom and told her I loved her and we had a wonderful conversation. Three weeks to the day of the word, my mom slipped into a coma in the hospital after having emergency surgery and died a few weeks later. Within a few months, all that the Lord promised would return had. I was thankful the Lord had given me the timing so that I could say goodbye. I was also deeply convinced that there are always consequences to approaching the prophetic through illegal channels. I don't know why the curse was not broken prior to her death, but I'm thankful that the Lord brought restoration.

PRAYER ACTIVATION

If you find yourself in a similar situation, repent on behalf of the occultist activity, cancel any curses and demonic assignments attached to the activity and pray blessing over yourself and your family members. Also, ask the Lord if there is anything else you need to pray or declare to right the situation. Journal any revelation here.

_____

_____

_____

_____

_____

_____

_____

_____

_____

_____

_____

_____

_____

The prophetic word from God carries the anointing to heal. A person can be healed from a lifelong trauma instantly by the revelation of the heart of God. I experienced healing in a dramatic encounter with one of the very first prophetic words I received. The prophet called me out with words of knowledge about God's perspective of my teenage years. He shared some very personal insights that instantly healed my heart. It was akin to undergoing emotional heart surgery. Not only was my heart restored, but also when I returned to the bed and breakfast my husband and I were staying at and looked in the mirror, I noticed my eyes were a different color. My eyes had always been a dull blue gray and now they were a bright green. The change was drastic. I asked the Lord about it and He said He had created me with bluish green eyes and that the pain of childhood had created layers of dull gray over top. Now that the pain was healed, my eyes sparkled like fine gemstones. My change in eye color later testified to my mom and best friend of the Lord's goodness. Signs that make you wonder! We owe the world an encounter with the One who loves us beyond all measure.

WHAT IS THE PROPHETIC?

The prophetic is God interacting with the world. He's always speaking, in the myriad of ways that He does. We can fine-tune our ability to hear and understand Him through relationship with Him and through studying His ways. In John 12:28-29, Father God spoke from Heaven about Jesus saying, "I have both glorified it (my Name) and will glorify it again." Jesus heard God's words clearly. Others standing by heard thunder and others thought an angel had spoken to Jesus. The word of the Father was clear but people's ability to hear Him depended upon their intimacy with Him. Jesus' relationship with His Father is a prototype for how we, too, as children of God can be in close relationship with Him. The more time we spend with God, the more clearly we will hear His voice.

Another key to interacting with Heaven is being baptized in the Holy Spirit. Jesus told His disciples to wait after His ascension for the promised outpouring of the Holy Spirit.

Acts 1:4-6, 8, "And being assembled together with them, He commanded them not to depart from Jerusalem, but to wait for the Promise of the Father, "which," He said, "you have heard from Me; for John truly baptized with the Holy Spirit not many days from now." "But you shall receive power when the Holy Spirit has come upon you; and you shall be witnesses to Me in Jerusalem, and in all Judea and Samaria, and to the end of the earth.""

The Holy Spirit was poured out on those who believed Jesus. Acts 2:2-4 records the account, "And suddenly there came a sound from heaven, as of a rushing mighty wind, and it filled the whole house where they were sitting. Then there appeared to them divided tongues, as of fire, and one sat upon each of them. And they were all filled with the Holy Spirit and began to speak with other tongues, as the Spirit gave them utterance."

The result of the Holy Spirit outpouring that day was a harvest of 3000 souls and the Gospel going forth into all the earth. If the disciples, who spent 3 ½ years walking closely with Jesus on the earth needed to be filled with the Holy Spirit, how much more do we need to now? Being filled with the Holy Spirit gives us hunger for deeper relationship with God, boldness for witnessing for Christ, power for accomplishing all that Jesus commanded we do, love for God, for ourselves and for others, the ability to hear from God more clearly, greater understanding of Scripture, and a spiritual prayer language to pray the perfect will of God. Speaking in tongues is one of the evidences of the baptism in the Holy Spirit. Praying in tongues will bring your spirit encouragement, joy, and enable the angels to accomplish God's will on your behalf. Believers need an initial infilling with the Holy Spirit that is subsequent to salvation and then need repeated refilling because we leak.

PRAYER ACTIVATION

God is faithful to fill us with His Holy Spirit when we ask. If you've never been filled with Holy Spirit or need a fresh baptism, now is a great time to ask the Lord the following:

Thank you, Father for sending Your Son to be my Lord and Savior. I also ask you for an infilling of your Holy Spirit. Fill me up, Lord. I receive all that You have for me. I, also, receive praying in tongues now. Please help me to speak in tongues for Your glory. Please help me to hear Your voice more clearly and understand Scripture. I love you. Amen.

Take some time to journal anything the Father shows you here.

_____

_____

_____

_____

_____

_____

_____

_____

_____

_____

_____

_____

_____

_____

_____

_____

_____

_____

_____

_____

CHAPTER 2

DNA OF PROPHETIC CULTURE

Our prophetic culture must be Love. Loving God well, loving ourselves and others well. Pure and simple love.

"And though I have the gift of prophecy, and understand all mysteries and all knowledge, and though I have all faith, so that I could remove mountains, but have not love, I am nothing. And though I bestow all my goods to feed the poor, and though I give my body to be burned, but have not love, it profits me nothing. Love suffers long and is kind; love does not envy; love does not parade itself, is not puffed up; does not behave rudely, does not seek its own, is not provoked, thinks no evil; does not rejoice in iniquity, but rejoices in the truth; bears all things, believes all things, hopes all things, endures all things. Love never fails." 1 Corinthians 13:2-8

Our goal in releasing the prophetic must be to honor people and by doing so, plant a seed for them to know the Living God. "But God demonstrates His own love toward us, in that while we were still sinners, Christ died for us." Romans 5:8

The nature of the prophetic anointing is intimacy. As we partner with God in giving a prophetic word, the Lord releases a fragrance from Heaven that draws people close. They lean in because their identity and purpose for being alive is being revealed. If we don't operate in love, that intimacy that draws them in becomes like a weapon that can maim them. Instead of the sweet kiss they were expecting, they are bitten. Many people have left the church wounded because of prophetic people who didn't use their gifting in love.

The prophetic is not used to correct or discipline people, especially never publicly. Correction and discipline, when needed, is done through relationship using wisdom and revelation from God, not through the delivery of a prophetic word. The Lord may show a leader a problem. When revelation is received, intercession is most often the proper response. At the direction of the Lord, someone may be corrected but it's not done through the guise of a prophetic word.

With the prophetic, we show people how God sees them, how He loves them and is proud of them. When my son was eight years old, God showed him and us what he's called to do in his lifetime. More importantly, God showed me how He honors my son. He already views him and treats him as the man he will become and all that he will accomplish. Even though my son was a little boy, Heaven respected him for his potential, no matter where he was in the process. It was insight to me into how God views all of us. He's not disappointed in us. He loves us and wants to encourage us. We have the awesome privilege of seeing through the lens of Heaven to inspire those around us to do and be all that they were created for.

One of my favorite testimonies of the power of the prophetic word to transform someone came from a word Prophet Kris Vallotton gave a homeless man years ago. Pastor Kris was preaching at Bethel Church in Redding when he saw God's heart for a man sitting in the congregation. Kris asked the man to stand and told him that God said he was a pillar in the house of God, one called to pastor God's children, an upright citizen and man of God. He continued with more details of the man's destiny. Anyone witnessing the word would have noticed that what God saw was a very different current reality in the man's life. The man was homeless, dirty, hopeless, and addicted to heroin. The man wept as he heard how God saw him and the plans He had for his life. A year later, a well-groomed man appeared to Kris and asked him if he remembered him. Kris confessed that he didn't. The man reminded Kris of the prophetic word from the year before. He told Kris that he was instantly delivered from a lifetime of drug abuse as he received the word of the Lord; he was employed, had a home, and was pursuing a relationship with Jesus. Through seeing through God's redemptive view of mankind, Kris released the ability for the man to become who he was designed to be.

POWER OF IMPARTATION

1 Timothy 4:14 explains how powerful impartation is for our development of spiritual gifts. The Apostle Paul reminded Timothy, "Do not neglect the gift that is in you, which was given to you by prophecy with the laying on of the hands of the eldership."

We can receive a gift through prayer, through prophetic word, through God divinely giving it to us, and through the laying on of hands. We may receive the gifting in infant form and as we are faithful in developing it, it will grow. Our gifting grows through use, faith and stewardship. I've received different flavors of gifting and increase in gifting through impartation. Stir up your faith to receive supernatural impartation and you'll reap the rewards.

There is no time or space differential in the spirit. The same prayer for healing that is released in a meeting can be viewed later by video and be received. As you read through this book, understand that what is released here through impartation can be yours by faith.

VIEW OF GOD

How we perceive God will be the lens through which we prophesy. If we view Him as an angry, distant father, our prophetic words will reflect that distortion. If we view the role of the Father as one of condemnation and punishment, we'll release bitter judgmental words that don't reflect love or the true heart of God.

Jesus said if we've seen Him, we've seen the Father (John 14:90). Jesus said He came to give life and life more abundantly (John 10:10). Romans 2:4 is a key to the proper filter for the prophetic: "Or do you despise the riches of His goodness, forbearance, and longsuffering, not knowing that the goodness of God leads you to repentance?"

Our job is to show people the kindness of God, the love of God. People who are walking in sin do so because of lies they're believing and wounds they've experienced. The true power of the prophetic releases truth, heals hearts and draws people into intimacy with their Creator.

FILTERS

Most of us grow up with ungodly beliefs that filter how we perceive the world. These filters can take many forms. Religious spirits, fear, rejection, judgment, lawlessness, control, a victim mindset, a belief that people are naughty and need punishment, and an unhealthy eschatology all contribute to us not seeing clearly.

The Apostle Paul tells us in Romans 12:2 "And do not be conformed to this world, but be transformed by the renewing of your mind, that you may prove what is that good and acceptable and perfect will of God."

Our minds get renewed and filters are removed from our perception when we read the Bible and when we spend time with God. It's a process as we walk with God. However, we want to be careful not to hurt other people as we walk towards our own freedom. That's why our pursuit of hearing and releasing the voice of God on the earth has to be rooted and grounded in the fact that God is a good, loving Father and our job is to be ministers of reconciliation between Heaven and earth.

So much of prophesying is about how we process and deliver the revelation we receive. The revelation comes pure from Heaven, but if it goes through a bad filter, it gets skewed and becomes toxic. I learned how important it is to not have filters firsthand through a bad experience with receiving a prophetic word from a prophet who had multiple bad filters. My husband and I were in a wilderness season where nothing seemed to go right. We had sold everything to follow God across the country when He called us. Shortly after, my husband lost his job and we were both scrambling to find work. Our extended family relationships were experiencing a lot of strain as a result of our season and other mitigating factors. And I was confused and pressing into hearing the voice of God for myself for answers to our problems, but wasn't successful. I went to a home group in another city, hoping to encounter the Lord. The prophet prayed for me and heard three things from the Lord: financial stress, family relationship problems, problems hearing God. The revelation was pure and accurate. However, he had a filter that said that people were naughty and didn't obey God so his word to me sounded like this:

"You're having financial problems because you won't do what the Lord is telling you to do. Because of your disobedience, you've hurt your extended family relationships and because you won't do what the Lord is telling you to do, you can't hear Him."

I felt like I'd been punched in the gut by that word. I was confused because the revelation was so accurate, yet was used to wound. That experience drove home to me the importance of how prophetic words are delivered. A healthy word that would have released encouragement and the heart of the Father to me would have used the same revelation but conveyed it like this:

"The Lord loves you and He wants you to know you can trust Him to be your provider, your Jehovah-Jireh. He sees your situation and is bringing about solutions for you. He cares about you and your family and will always provide. He's also working behind the scenes and has a plan to restore your extended family relationships. There's a Lamb for a family. His sacrifice will bring healing to your family, too. He'll protect your heart as He provides for you. Times where it is hard to hear His voice can be because you're tucked up so tightly under the shadow of the Almighty. He's with you, Annie. He promises that He'll never leave you or forsake you. You can trust Him. He is good and has your situation. I pray for God to restore your finances. I cancel any demonic assignments against you and your family regarding finances and relationships and I pray that you can always hear His voice. His sheep hear His voice and He stands behind and orders your steps. I bless you to hear from your Father. In Jesus name, amen."

If the word had been delivered like that, the fruit of it would have been peace and trust. In addition, the angels would have been activated to accomplish the word of the Lord. The kindness of the Lord empowers. Even if I had been at fault regarding my situation, the heart of God released in love brings about repentance and a change of direction. We can trust the Holy Spirit to convict where it is necessary and we can just be agents of love as we prophesy His solutions.

PRAYER ACTIVATION

Pray and ask God what filters you may have or any view of God that skews your ability to receive pure revelation from Him. Examples may include: religious/Pharisee spirit, control, judgment, rejection, victim mentality, lawlessness, fear, negative eschatology, people need to be punished, taking on Holy Spirit's job of conviction of sin, and others. Ask Him to expose lies you've believed, reveal truth to renew your mind, heal any wounds you may have. Use the allotted space to journal and write truth.

_____

_____

_____

_____

_____

_____

_____

_____

Annie Blouin

CHAPTER 3

OLD TESTAMENT PROPHETIC VS NEW TESTAMENT PROPHETIC

The story of mankind was written before man was created. Father God, Jesus and Holy Spirit desired to be in close relationship with man and woman. Humankind was designed for intimacy. The story of mankind is a love story. Love between Creator and created. The Trinity had a plan for redemption before mankind was born or had ever sinned.

Paul in Ephesians 1:4 describes this by saying, "just as He chose us in Him before the foundation of the world, that we should be holy and without blame before Him in love,". Love is woven through the Old Testament and the New Testament.

The message of the Old Testament is that man is in need of a Savior and that the One is coming to deliver and redeem back into relationship. Man cannot through good works save himself. Jesus is the bridge to the Father. The harshness of the Old Testament is revealing the need for a Savior. Mankind in its wickedness demanded the Law and then failed to keep it. The Father throughout the Old Testament continued rescuing His people from slavery, wooing them to His heart, and declaring through His prophets that a better Covenant was coming. King David's revelation in the Old Testament was that God wanted relationship and not sacrifice. David was ahead of his time in understanding worship and intimacy with the Father. As people of the New Testament Covenant, we have to understand that the purpose of the prophetic in the Old Testament was to point people to the revelation that they were sinners in need of a Savior. The only people who could hear the voice of God were the prophets and the Jewish kings. The voice of God through the prophets was a message of repentance.

The message of the New Testament prophetic is that we have a Savior available for us and He loves us. Every Believer has the Holy Spirit living inside and has the ability to hear the voice of God himself. It's the Holy Spirit's job to convict people of sin and their need for a Savior, not ours. Our message to the world is that Jesus loves them and came to save them. It's not the severe message that the Old Testament conveyed, but rather a wooing message to the hearts of those not yet in relationship with the King of kings and Lord of lords. We'd be wise to hear the tone of love coming from Heaven and release love through the prophetic voice we carry as Believers. We can trust the Holy Spirit to do His multiple jobs of conviction, wooing, preparing hearts, and many others. We can then focus on our job of releasing the love of the Father for His children.

<u>Old Testament Prophetic- only through the prophets</u>

Bring Repentance

Reveal and Expose Sin

Bring Judgment

Reveal Secrets

Counsel Kings

Set People in Leadership

Signs & Wonders

Shock & Awe

Interpret Dreams

New Testament Prophetic- through all Believers and even the unsaved

Reveal Love

Reveal Truth

Call out the Gold in People

Reveal Identity, Purpose and Calling

Draw People to God

Bring Heaven to Earth

Signs & Wonders

Miracles & Healings

Reveal a Loving Father

Counsel

Exhort, Edify, Encourage, Comfort

Reveal Strategy

Bring Hope

Remove Mountains/Roadblocks

Bless

Help People Transition

Birth Dreams

Interpret Dreams

Protect

Release Provision from Heaven

Cancel Assignments of the Demonic

Release Heaven's Justice for People

PRAYER ACTIVATION

Take some time here to pray through any misunderstandings you've had over the role of the New Testament prophetic. Ask God to heal any wounds you've experienced through others. Ask Him to reveal truth to you and to illuminate your understanding of the Word. Use the space provided to journal.

_____

_____

_____

_____

_____

_____

_____

_____

_____

_____

_____

_____

END TIMES ESCHATOLOGY

How we view where we are on the time clock of history has everything to do with how we live. Jesus told us to occupy by building His kingdom until He returns. Our job of Kingdom building is clear. Believers for the past 2000 years believed in building until the early 20th century. At that point, Christians became convinced that Jesus' return was imminent. The problem with that thought process is when Believers exit the leadership role in the earth, the landscape of society changes drastically to reflect the kingdom of darkness. Many Christians removed themselves from the 7 mountains of influence, particularly education, government and Hollywood. With Believers not fully engaged on the scene, the enemy was happy to step in to educate the children of future generations, change laws away from righteousness, and change culture through films and media. Christians are the leaven for righteousness in this world and we need to lead and influence leaders. The 1946 movie "It's a Wonderful Life" with Jimmy Stewart models this principle well. In the movie, Stewart's character decides he doesn't want to live and doesn't think he's made a difference in the world because of his small town existence and influence. An angel appears and shows him what his town would have looked like without Stewart's leadership and influence. The town is dark; full of debauchery and poverty. Stewart has an epiphany as he walks around the shady town of how important bringers of light are, regardless of how seemingly mindless their existence appears.

Believers are salt and light for this world. We can't get caught up in the mindset that the world is getting darker and Jesus is going to show up at any moment to rescue us from the planet. Jesus is coming back for a victorious, conquering Bride. It is not the nature of the Creator of the Universe, the Almighty Father, to let the enemy destroy the planet. We were created to be kings, serving THE King, to bring His kingdom to earth. On earth as it is in Heaven, our Lord taught us.

In the late 1990s, immediately after getting saved, I read the "Left Behind" series by Tim LaHaye and Jerry Jenkins. The series confirmed to me that choosing Jesus was a wise decision, however, it discouraged me about not having a future or a hope. I almost chose not to have children because I thought that Jesus would return before they had a chance to grow up. That thought process also caused me to make decisions that didn't contribute to being salt or light in my community. Fortunately, God began to speak to me and show me the future He had for me. He told me I would live a long life and showed me some things my children would accomplish for Him many decades in the future.

To settle this in your heart, I highly recommend reading "Victorious Eschatology" by Harold Eberle. He does an in depth study of Scripture related to the Kingdom age that we're in and it's an optimistic view of the future. He explains the history of the Scriptures that are used by eschatologists for a rapture escape at any moment from the planet and illuminates God's plan for now.

If Jesus were to return today, many billions of souls would spend eternity in hell because they haven't yet chosen Him. The enemy would like to speed up the clock to capture more of God's chosen, but Jesus is patient; patient that all would hear the Gospel and would have time to choose. I don't even know if modern day theologians have correctly interpreted Scripture regarding the end time battle. John the Revelator, had trouble describing what he saw, much less interpreting it. I do know that we're not at the end yet. We're in the Kingdom building age and we need to focus on being light and salt and not be distracted by the enemy's plans.

PRAYER ACTIVATION

Pray through any end times eschatology you have that doesn't line up with the mandate for Believers to build the kingdom until Jesus returns. Use the space here to examine your beliefs.

_____

_____

_____

_____

_____

_____

_____

_____

_____

_____

_____

_____

_____

WHERE REVELATION COMES FROM

SCRIPTURE

Revelation from Heaven comes in many forms. In the next chapter, we'll talk about the primary ways God speaks that supplement His Word. The Bible says we worship God in spirit and in truth. We connect to Him as spirits and also can experience Him in our souls and bodies. As we read Scripture, the Holy Spirit illuminates it for our understanding. We've all experienced times when Scripture seems to jump off the page and we know that God is speaking to us directly. Scripture can also contradict itself, not on moral principles, but on direction. One verse can state something and the very next verse can say the reverse principle.

For example, Proverbs 26:4, "Do not answer a fool according to his folly, lest you also be like him". And then immediately following, the exact opposite principle in Proverbs 26:5, "Answer a fool according to his folly, lest he be wise in his own eyes".

Which one is correct? Both are. Scripture was never meant to be interpreted outside of relationship with the Holy Spirit. As we journey through our Bibles, the Holy Spirit is our guide.

SPIRITUAL AIRWAVES

Spiritual airwaves exist throughout the world. They are similar to radio waves where people can hear what is being broadcast through thoughts and feelings by both the heavenly realm and the demonic realm. God's plan for cities and people groups will be broadcast in an area to create atmospheres. People hear it mostly unconsciously in their thoughts. For example, God created the people in the Midwestern regions of America to be strong, hard working, and full of integrity, among many other attributes. Simultaneously, the enemy is broadcasting distorting thoughts such as people's identities and worth are based on whether or not they've been productive enough that day, that they're only valuable if they are really intelligent, and that they have to earn love by their efforts. When people in the Midwest have an orphan spirit, they strive for identity and love. Contrarily, throughout the world, when people are secure in their identity as sons and daughters of the Most High God, they dismiss what the enemy is broadcasting and embrace what they're hearing in God's airwaves.

Different areas of the nation and world have different airwaves. In California, God broadcasts leadership, innovation, freedom, joy and play. The enemy broadcasts a Peter Pan syndrome, narcissism, irresponsibility, sexual immorality, and others. Depending on which kingdom people tune into will determine their beliefs and their actions.

People who are spiritually sensitive can feel/hear the airwaves/atmospheres on more of a conscious level than others. These "feelers" can drive down a road and feel the culture of an office building, a street, a neighborhood, a state line, individual homes, etc. All of that input can be very tiring and feels like a roller coaster ride for someone who is so in tune. The way that people can maintain the peace and joy of the Lord is to first know his/her identity as a son/daughter of Christ. Secondly, take every thought/feeling captive to the obedience of Christ.

II Corinthians 10:3-5 explains this concept to us, "For though we walk in the flesh, we do not war according to the flesh. For the weapons of our warfare are not carnal but mighty in God for pulling down strongholds, casting down arguments and every high thing that exalts itself against the knowledge of God, bringing every thought into captivity to the obedience of Christ."

This requires knowing the truth about who God says we are. Reading the Word daily keeps this truth in us and in front of us so that we can recognize the thoughts that don't line up with Scripture. Thirdly, carry our own open heaven. Be aware of the Presence of the Lord and keep that relationship in the forefront of our day. Jacob had a dream where he saw the angels ascending and descending above him. It opened his eyes to the reality that he could carry an open heaven with him where God's purposes are accomplished (Genesis 28:12).

There is a constant battle between God's kingdom and Satan's kingdom for people and for control of the airwaves in regions. The angels are empowered to establish the Kingdom of God when the people of God worship, pray, walk in righteousness, and commune with God. The demons are empowered through sin, contention, lack of Believers' light, and other things.

One of my favorite cities on the planet is Washington, D.C. I love walking around the city feeling the hopes and plans of God for our nation. The tangible presence of the Lord is very strong around the city and the Presidential monuments. God loves our nation and is very vested in our destiny and future. In 2015, I visited D.C. in January, April and July. In January and July, I didn't notice anything untoward in the airwaves; however, April felt and sounded like a war zone. The Supreme Court was deciding a ruling on gay marriage, due in June. The battle was on in the spiritual realm. As I walked around, I heard in the spirit clear as day the arguments for legalizing gay marriage, "It should be okay for people to choose whom they love. What's wrong with people loving whomever they want to? You're intolerant and not loving if you deny people the right to marry whom they choose." I didn't hear any Biblical truth being released in the airwaves that week and knew the 9 Supreme Court Justices were also hearing subconsciously what was being broadcast in the spirit. I knew at that time what their decision would be in June.

Believers have an interesting road to walk regarding homosexuality. The Bible clearly says homosexuality is a perversion. The reason is because any sexuality outside of covenant in marriage brings people in bondage to the enemy. God hates that His children suffer when they sin. The culture of America by legalizing gay marriage just became more oppressed. What people need is an encounter with a loving God. The kindness of God brings repentance and releases people into freedom. As Believers, we need to release love and not judgment, so that they can find the God who loves them beyond all measure. And it's our job to pray, release light and worship and righteousness to empower the angelic to win with what's released in the airwaves.

PRAYER ACTIVATION

In the space provided, examine any beliefs you hold that don't line up with Scripture that you may have heard in the airwaves in your region. Spend time daily in the Word of God to renew your mind.

_____

_____

_____

_____

_____

_____

_____

_____

CHAPTER 4

WAYS GOD SPEAKS

God speaks in a multitude of ways and is always stretching us to expand our understanding. One way He communicates with us is through our fifteen spiritual senses. I'll teach here on the first five, which correspond with our five natural senses. If you're interested in learning about the other ten spiritual senses, Dan McCollam of The Mission Church in Vacaville, California explains them well.

5 SPIRITUAL SENSES

God shows us His kingdom to help us interact more with Him. He wants us to know Him more and is happy to show us His kingdom. The Holy Spirit shows us certain aspects of the demonic so that we can know what is keeping us in bondage and can dialogue with Him for the keys to freedom.

TASTE

Taste and see that the Lord is good. The Lord's Presence can be discerned through taste. I haven't personally experienced this yet; however, people will taste sweet things, similar to honey when the Lord's presence is strong. The presence of the demonic can be discerned through a metallic taste or other foul tastes.

SMELL

We can smell both kingdoms. Even though we smell it through our nose, it's not a natural smell. It's a spiritual smell that we discern through our spiritual sense of smell. Unless you're aware that it's a spiritual smell, it will be just like smelling something with your physical nose. Twice, I've smelled Jesus as a smell similar to roses, but stronger. The first time was in the middle of a worship service and when the Presence of God got really strong, a beautiful fragrance accompanied it. The second time was on a night prayer walk. He's so beautiful to behold!

The demonic also carries different smells that can be discerned through our spiritual nose. The spirit of infirmity (illness/disease) smells like mildew/mold. The spirit of cancer/death smells like sewer waste. The spirit of addiction smells like cigarettes. A pastor friend of mine who visits people in jail is able to discern what drugs they use by the demonic smell of drugs. He says that the demon attached to cocaine use smells different than the one attached to heroin use.

PRAYER ACTIVATION

Take a moment to pray and journal any experiences you've had with experiencing God through your spiritual sense of taste and smell. Ask Him to activate these for you so that you can encounter Him and be set free from anything holding you in bondage that you're not aware of.

_____

_____

_____

_____

_____

_____

_____

_____

_____

_____

_____

_____

_____

FEELING

God communicates to us through our physical sense of feeling. God will give us goose bumps on our arms, and sometimes legs, when He's calibrating truth for us. It helps us to build faith in what we're learning or discussing or hearing when He confirms it through the physical sensation of goose bumps. I've experienced sharing testimonies of God's miracle healing power with people and God will confirm it is truth through giving them a tangible sensation. He uses that impression as a sign and a wonder confirming His word. Another way God communicates through physical feeling is heat. The Bible says that Believers are to lay hands on the sick and that they will recover (Mark 16:17-18). There is a supernatural transfer of God's healing from the Believer's hands into the sick person when hands are laid on the sick. Often this healing feels like electricity and/or heat. The person's body often feels hot in that area as the healing is accomplished.

The angels like to participate in bringing about God's purposes on earth. Often, when God is healing trauma in a person, angels will gently touch the person's head in the place where the trauma resides in the brain. This brings healing and rewires the neuro pathways and thought process for the person. The person may or may not feel the gentle healing touch in their head. Angels likewise operate in this manner when a person is renewing their mind through believing the Word of God.

We can discern God's Presence and angelic presence through feeling vibrations or frequencies in the air through our feeler spiritual sense. The vibrations angels emit is similar to what it feels like being in a hot tub when the jets are turned on. The frequency will feel like it is being emitted in waves. The Holy Spirit feels similar to the angels, but the wavelength is shorter and stronger. It feels heavy and peaceful.

The demonic is also discerned through feeling. A spirit of witchcraft or control can be felt in an area by a person experiencing dizziness. Dizziness obviously has natural, physical causes but when it's experienced through a spiritual sense of feeling the cause is discernment of a witchcraft spirit. Just because someone is sensitive enough to discern a spirit, does not mean that they're assigned to do anything with it. Instead, it invites dialogue with the Lord over it. A very sensitive person will feel a lot and through maturity learns to focus in on what the Lord is doing and to ignore the rest.

Another sign of the demonic being present is a room or an area of a room being unnaturally cold. The temperature of the room may even indicate it's 72 degrees, but the space will feel icy. We've experienced that twice in two different homes. After praying through the rooms, they returned to room temperature feel because the icy presence left.

In dangerous situations, people can feel a wave of fear come over them that they're discerning with their spiritual sense of feel. People talk about the hair on the back of their neck standing up when they can't see danger, yet they feel its presence. Tuning into the Lord in those moments can make the difference between safety and tragedy.

I'll address the various ways of feeling more in the next section of the 4 primary ways God speaks.

PRAYER ACTIVATION

In the space provided, journal events you've experienced with your spiritual feeling sense. Ask God to show you what His world is like. Ask Him to activate your feeling sense and pray that the demonic does not use any of your senses to parade before you.

_____

_____

_____

_____

_____

_____

_____

_____

_____

_____

_____

_____

_____

_____

_____

HEARING

Hearing God speak through our spiritual ears ranges from the thoughts of the Holy Spirit to the external audible voice of God.

EXTERNAL AUDIBLE VOICE

The external audible voice is rare and others around us may or may not hear it, too. God speaks audibly when there is danger or when we need to hear Him very clearly. God spoke from Heaven over Jesus about glorifying His name in John 12:28-29. Some heard what was spoken but thought an angel said it. Some didn't hear it and others heard thunder. The closer we are in relationship to God, the more clearly we hear Him speak in the multitude of ways He chooses.

INTERNAL AUDIBLE VOICE

This sounds like the audible voice of God inside your head. It sounds loud, like God clearly said something to you. It is unmistakably inside your head and you don't wonder if anyone around you heard it. God may ask you something in the form of a question and then answer the question. When He speaks this way, it is often a suddenly and interrupts what you were thinking about and may or may not be related to what you were pondering.

This is my favorite way for God to communicate with me because there is no doubt about what He said. It always gives me a thrill of experiencing Heaven invading earth. I treasure these moments and always record them in my journal. Hearing God's internal audible voice does not happen as frequently as I would like in my life. When He speaks in the internal audible voice, I can trust what He has said is true and will come to pass. I often hear Him speak in the internal audible voice when I'm asleep. He regularly gives me direction during the nighttime in that manner. In the summer of 2014, we knew God was moving us back across the country but we weren't sure of the timing. We thought we would have moved in 2013 and didn't, so we were cautious by the time the next summer arrived. I knew He'd told me earlier that when we did move, He wanted me to homeschool my children. By late July 2014, even though He hadn't yet confirmed we were moving soon, He told me during the night to get off the homeschool fence and prepare to homeschool beginning late August. A week later, He confirmed the move and we moved in early

September. So much of relationship with God is about trusting Him and His leading.

STILL SMALL VOICE

When God speaks to us in the still small voice, we can often miss what He said if we're not tuned in. The still small voice is subtle, and quiet. God likes to stretch us in learning to hear Him. Commonly, after hearing Him speak in the still small voice, you'll question whether you heard Him correctly. Keep pressing in. He's worth it!

THOUGHTS FROM THE HOLY SPIRIT

The Holy Spirit often communicates with us through putting thoughts in our head. We don't "hear" it per say, rather, it sounds like a thought that pops into our head. We need to learn to differentiate the thoughts in our head that are our thoughts, the enemy's thoughts, and the Holy Spirit's thoughts. The Holy Spirit will never contradict the Bible. Studying the Bible is key to our recognizing the voice of the Lord. Often the Holy Spirit will put a thought in our head in the form of a question. This is an invitation to dialogue with Him about the answer.

NABI' FLOW

Nabi' flow prophetic means "to bubble forth". We access this type of prophetic through faith. Faith that God wants to speak and share His heart at any time. The seer realm requires waiting on God for revelation and interpretation, whereas, the Nabi' flow is activated through belief. Prophecy is often through the Nabi' flow prophetic. As we approach God with faith, He gives us a word. We often "hear" with the Nabi' flow. Then, as we speak what we've received, the Lord will continue giving us more for the person we're ministering to. It is the fastest type of prophesying. It bubbles up inside of us and flows out as we have the courage to speak. Often, it starts as one word and won't progress until that word is shared.

PRAYER ACTIVATION

Journal encounters you've had with the Lord through hearing Him. Have you experienced all of the aforementioned ways to hear the Lord? Anytime the Lord shows you something, He likes to show you more and often will if you ask Him questions about what He's said.

_____

_____

_____

_____

_____

_____

_____

_____

_____

_____

_____

_____

_____

_____

_____

_____

SEEING

Seeing in the spiritual realm ranges from seeing visions with our eyes wide open to seeing slight impressions in our mind's eye. One type of vision is not more valuable than another. However, we tend to remember the open visions more because they leave more of an impact upon us. God uses the screen of our imagination to speak to us through "seeing". If I tell you to envision a pink elephant right now, you can see it on the screen of your imagination.

OPEN VISIONS

An open vision is like watching a movie unfold in front of your eyes with your natural eyes open. You can still see and hear whatever is in the natural background, as well. The vision can last anywhere from one second in time to many minutes or more. The Lord uses open visions to communicate things to us that He wants to go deep in our spirits or we may see them when we're prophesying over someone and the Lord wants us to see the backstory or the future quickly. The seer realm can either be literal or symbolic. Visions tend to be more literal than pictures and impressions. Pictures and impressions are often symbolic and need an interpretation. Whether literal or symbolic, the Lord invites us to dialogue with Him about what we see. We can have an open vision when we're asleep. It will appear to us as though it were a dream, but unlike a dream that needs interpreting, a night vision will most often be literal.

Acts 10:9-16 recounts the story of the Apostle Peter's vision of the Lord showing him that it's okay for him to eat meat. The Lord's voice accompanied the vision, giving literal instruction. "The next day, as they went on their journey and drew near the city, Peter went up on the housetop to pray, about the sixth hour. Then he became very hungry and wanted to eat; but while they made ready, he fell into a trance and saw heaven opened and an object like a great sheet bound at the four corners, descending to him and let down to the earth. In it were all kinds of four-footed animals of the earth, wild beasts, creeping things, and birds of the air. And a voice came to him, "Rise, Peter; kill and eat." But Peter said, "Not so, Lord! For I have never eaten anything common or unclean." And a voice spoke to him again the second time, "What God has cleansed you must not call common." This was done three times. And the object was taken up into heaven again." Even as the vision was occurring, Peter was dialoguing with the Lord to get understanding because it was such a paradigm shift for him as a Jewish man.

My first open vision occurred one night in 2005 as I was in my room praying. I was talking to the Lord, when suddenly, a movie scene started playing a few feet in front of me. In the first scene, I saw Father God crying and watching Jesus' journey to the Cross. I felt the Father's heart of love for Jesus and His people and His sorrow at the suffering Jesus was experiencing. Then the scene changed and I saw Jesus on His way to the Cross, looking at me with such love in His eyes as He was beaten and crucified. I felt His heart that He would willingly suffer to reconcile me to the Father. He told me He loved me and died for me. His love for me became extremely personal. The scene changed one final time and I saw the Father crying as He watched painful events from my childhood and adolescence. He was showing me His heart for me as traumatic scenes from my life flashed on the screen. The Father's love and compassion for me undid me. The why of the pain no longer mattered; my heart understood that He was always with me and His presence and compassion in my life was what was important. The entire vision lasted less than a minute, but it changed me. It rooted me in the Father's love like nothing up to that point had. I will forever cherish that gift from my Father.

PRAYER ACTIVATION

Take some time to reflect on any open visions you've had and journal here. Ask the Lord to give you His eyes to see and ask Him to speak to you in visions.

_____

_____

_____

_____

_____

_____

_____

_____

_____

_____

_____

CLOSED VISIONS

These are visions that run like movies on the screen of your mind's eye. They're often short, a second or so in length. You can miss them if you don't recognize what they are. Often the Lord gives instruction to help solve problems you've been praying about in closed visions. I was experiencing trouble writing chapter one of this manual and asked the Lord for help. Throughout the day as I was writing, I saw 3-4 times a quick closed vision of me taking Communion and asking people to cover the project in prayer. I finally realized those were closed visions and that was the solution I needed. Fortunately, the Lord repeated the visions until I received the revelation. I acted on both of those directives and experienced a shift in ease of writing.

PRAYER ACTIVATION

Ask the Lord to reveal any closed visions He's given you that you've missed and ask Him to train your spirit in communicating with Him in visions. Journal any thoughts here.

_____

_____

_____

_____

_____

_____

_____

_____

_____

PICTURES

These are given on the screen of your imagination. They are similar to closed visions except they are a still picture. They're also very fast, and can flash across your screen in microseconds. Just like the burning bush that Moses saw, he had to turn towards it to receive the encounter. We have to recognize that a picture from the Lord came in and turn our hearts towards the Lord to dialogue with Him about it. Pictures are mainly symbolic in nature, so they require an interpretation from the Lord. The exception to this can be someone who is very literal and prophesies specific, direct words. A literal person will often get literal pictures. By nature, the seer realm requires waiting on the Lord for revelation. Recently, a friend asked me for a season word for her. I told her I would ask the Lord. Later in the day as I was walking down the stairs, I saw a flash of a bridge. I knew the picture was for my friend and I knew it meant she was in a transition time, going from one place to another.

IMPRESSIONS

These are very similar to pictures. They're fast, but may be more of a concept than a picture. It may be a knowing that you saw on the screen of your imagination. Another friend asked me for a word. We live across the country from one another and we hadn't been in contact for a while, so I didn't know any current natural details in her life. I prayed for a few days and kept getting very slight impressions that she was moving and changing her children's school. The impressions were very subtle. I was hesitant to give her such a directive word with such a slight impression but finally wrote her the word. She wrote back to say they were moving in a few weeks and asked me for more details. I prayed into it and saw where she was moving and gave her a few more life specifics. She wrote back to say it was exactly where they were moving and felt the confirmation was a kiss from God. It wasn't revelation she didn't already know, but gave her the confidence to move into the new location knowing God was with her.

The screen of our imagination is an important communication tool with Heaven. It's important that we don't get our screen dirty and miss what the Lord is doing. Pornography and sexual sin compromise the screen that God shows us His kingdom on. If you're involved in sexual sin, repent and ask God for help in being released from bondage. Ask Him for the keys to purity in your life and ask Him to cleanse your imagination so that you can hear from Him more clearly. Reading the Bible cleanses us and the screens of our imagination.

Ephesians 5:25-26 illustrates this by saying, "just as Christ also loved the church and gave Himself for her, that He might sanctify and cleanse her with the washing of water by the word."

PRAYER ACTIVATION

Ask the Lord to speak to you more with pictures and impressions. Take some time to practice receiving from Him in this way. Journal what you receive here.

_____

_____

_____

_____

_____

_____

_____

_____

_____

_____

_____

_____

_____

_____

_____

_____

_____

_____

_____

_____

CHAPTER 5

4 PRIMARY WAYS GOD SPEAKS

We hear God through our intimacy with Him. We prophesy to people out of the relationship we carry with God. Most people will primarily communicate with God and be fluent in one of the following four ways of hearing, seeing, feeling and knowing. However, a person can learn all of the ways He communicates and be competent in each area. Particularly when God speaks to you as you're prophesying over someone, always ask Him for more about what He initially showed you and He'll typically show you more detail. The investigative questions of who, what, why, where, when, and how are helpful to use in dialoguing with the Lord. Also, this manual is equipping you in the basics and principles for hearing from the Lord but understand that God will not be put in a box. As soon as we make a rule for Him, He may show us the exception because He does not want our pursuit of Him to become religious form instead of a focus on relationship.

HEARING

Earlier in the previous chapter, I outlined the various ways to hear the Lord. Whatever way God speaks to you that you hear in each instance, it's an invitation for Him to show you more. I often get direction from the Lord through hearing. As we were transitioning to leave Redding, California, we moved out of a house and into an apartment in Redding. We knew we were leaving Redding but didn't know when. The first week we lived in the apartment, God spoke to me and said we would only live in the apartment for 6 months.

Sure enough, events unfolded and we moved across the country 6 months later.

SEEING

Again, earlier I outlined the major ways of seeing. The seer gifting of receiving from God requires waiting on the Lord and mostly requires an interpretation because of the symbolism involved in the seer realm. You can receive from the Lord during the day or the night. When you receive a picture from the Lord as you're prophesying, ask Him what it represents for them. If you see a picture of a waterfall or a rainbow, don't tell them you see a waterfall or rainbow for them. That's not a prophetic word. The word is the interpretation of the picture and if the picture is just a clue to getting the word, generally you don't need to share the picture. A lot of people get a picture and go to great lengths to describe all of the details of the picture and at the end of the amazing description, the person receiving the word has no more clarification on what the Lord is saying to them than before the picture was given. You also can't assume that when you see an airplane that it means that they are traveling somewhere, which is one meaning of airplanes in seer language. You have to ask God. Remember, He wants relationship with you and the person you're prophesying over, not formulas. God tends to speak to people in language that means something to them so always check with Him for the tone, flavor and nuances that He wants to communicate His love for them with the word.

The seer realm takes practice to develop into maturity. The more you practice, the faster you'll get at receiving pictures and interpretations and be able to deliver a skilled word that releases God's heart and grace in a person's life.

In reality, prophesying over someone is not usually limited to just one of the ways God speaks. You may see a picture and then hear an interpretation and then "know" something or "feel" something. We flow back and forth as we communicate with the Lord. Learning the seer realm symbolism can help build a vocabulary that God can speak to you through. I recommend Barbie Breathitt's "Dream Encounter Symbols". She studied under John Paul

Jackson and has a complete set of symbols that I've found helpful.

I'm a very literal and direct person. God made me that way so He mostly speaks to me through the seer realm in literal meanings and not symbolic. Even a lot of my dreams are literal and not symbolic. I had a dream about a friend in Redding where I was prophesying over her. I told her four direct words and the timing. I told her it was time to get married, time to buy a house, time to begin writing and time to be established as a prophet. When I awoke, I asked God if the words I had given her in the dream were literal and if I should deliver the word to her. He said yes, so I wrote her a message relaying those four words. She immediately responded in tears, saying she had been asking the Lord confirmation and timing for those four things in her life! She received the word and the accompanying grace. Five weeks later, she got married and bought a house, and began writing.

DISCERNMENT

Discernment is comprised of the gift of discerning of spirits (1Corinithians 12:10). It is discerning what the Holy Spirit is doing, what man's spirit is doing, and what the angelic and demonic spirits are doing. Discernment is further separated into communicating with God through "knowing" and "feeling". Discernment needs to be calibrated correctly so that a person is accurate with what they know and feel. Talking to mature people, without gossiping, can help discernment grow. It's also a gifting that people who operate in need to be connected to people in relationship in the Body of Christ so that the enemy doesn't isolate them and cause paranoia and suspicion. Wisdom is needed when helping children grow in this gifting so that they are not burdened by seeing and feeling too much too soon. The response of always checking in with the Lord and remembering that His burden is easy and His yoke is light and remembering that He doesn't call us to carry burdens is important.

KNOWING

People who flow in "knowing" from God will often know things about people. What they know seems obvious to everyone, but it's not. What they discern comes from Heaven and isn't instinctual and common. They will also just know direction from God, know what steps to take, know what God is doing in a situation. These people do not feel strongly prophetic because they believe what they know is just part of how they think and process. While they may be very intelligent and full of wisdom, things they "know" come from God and isn't just natural knowledge. They often flow very easily in the spiritual gifts of word of knowledge, word of wisdom and discerning of spirits. I'll describe these gifts in further detail in a later chapter. Information that comes in through "knowing" can just be there, without the person experiencing receiving it or it can drop in at a moment in time. Either way is valid. People who function in "knowing" need to periodically check in with God to be sure He hasn't changed the direction that they last knew was right in what they're building. People who are apostolic in nature often function in this manner. If you relate to this method of communicating with God, your prophetic gifting will work the best by you speaking what you "know" over people. It will encourage them. You'll also find that you intuitively know timing so prophesy timing as well over them.

This gift functions in my life mostly for transitions that people are in. I will suddenly "know" that someone is moving, or pregnant, or dying soon, or changing jobs, or getting married. I always check in with God when I know something if I'm to pray about it for them, pray to change it, or give them a word and release the grace to them for their transition.

PRAYER ACTIVATION

Ask the Lord to increase your ability to receive from Him through "knowing". Journal what He highlights as things He's already shown you through this gifting.

_____

_____

_____

_____

_____

_____

_____

_____

_____

_____

_____

_____

_____

FEELING

The supernatural ability to "feel" what's in an environment is a gift from the Lord to help bring Heaven to earth and release His solutions. I believe it's the hardest gifting to bring to maturity and until someone is mature, it is a gift that can make the person feel like they are on an emotional rollercoaster. Being aware through supernatural feeling is one of the most powerful tools to discern truth and one that brings great destruction to the enemy's plans. Feelers acutely feel what's in the airwaves. Many feelers, because of traumatic youth experiences, learn to use their gifting for self-protection. They use their awareness to dictate their actions and often become reactive to dangerous situations.

Even before I knew the Lord, my feeling gift was active and I used it to protect myself. Years after getting saved, the Lord asked me if I wanted to connect my discernment to the

Holy Spirit. Even though I knew my answer should be yes, I momentarily said no. I was afraid that if I wasn't aware of everything around me, I would be hurt. He showed me that He would protect me if I would let Him. I told Him I would trust Him and prayed to connect my discernment to the Holy Spirit. He showed me that without my discernment being connected to Him, the enemy used my gifting to ride in on with a spirit of fear and other things. My awareness of the environment quieted down significantly after I let the Lord protect me.

A feeler can feel when someone is sad, full of faith, excited, depressed and many other things because they can feel their atmosphere. They can feel someone's anointing, personality, favor, power, and temptations. They may be able to distinguish between what is in their generational line and what began in their life. They can feel what the Holy Spirit is doing in a room and in a person. A feeler can also feel angelic and demonic assignments, locations, and purposes. They can feel corporate culture, city identity, neighborhood characteristics and many other things.

The purpose of being able to feel is to connect with God to bring His plans to earth. Anytime I feel something, I've learned to quickly sort through it by asking God if it's my assignment or if I just became aware of it. Feeling is like radar that picks up a signal. If there is a lot in an environment, I'll focus in on what the Lord is doing. That helps quiet down the other information. Seers also have to do this if they see really well into a spiritual environment. I'm convinced that a large number of people who are diagnosed with mental illness are seers and feelers who aren't aware that they have a spiritual gift. As directed, a main purpose of feeling is to change it in intercession with the Lord or to shift it through declaration or a prophetic word. If you're feeling really distracted by all of the input in the spiritual realm, cleaning your house and organizing your physical environment can help bring order. Praying in tongues also releases a lot of peace into your environment.

My gifting has developed to the point where I can look at a map of a city I've never visited and I can "feel" the atmosphere in different locations and neighborhoods. When we moved to Raleigh, NC, I "felt" the map and chose Wake Forest because it not only felt good to me, but also felt like somewhere our family belonged. We were so confident in what I "felt", we rented a townhome online and moved sight unseen without visiting the city first.

As feelers, we can shift atmospheres and environments through releasing God's kingdom without ever saying a word. A few months ago, I was in Starbucks preparing teaching notes for the prophetic class I was teaching at our church's school of revival. As I sat there listening to worship music through my headphones, I noticed a strong demonic spirit of lust with the young man who had just sat down next to me. Two young women were with him and all three soon began talking about their collegiate sexual exploits. I continued working for a few minutes but didn't like how the atmosphere had shifted in the spirit. Without looking up from my work, I started pushing the Holy Spirit and purity with my spirit in their direction. I did this by sending my atmosphere to them. It took about 15 seconds for them to stop talking, gather their things and for them to leave the coffee shop. After they left, I finally looked up and saw one of the women outside the window staring at me. She knew that whatever had just happened had come from me because she "felt" the shift and where it came from. I pray that the Lord has continued wooing them for their hearts.

PRAYER ACTIVATION

If you've never connected your discernment gift of knowing and feeling to the Holy Spirit, now is a great time to pray that He will only show you what He wants you to know and that the enemy cannot parade before you. Journal any experiences with knowing and feeling that you've had.

_____

_____

_____

_____

_____

_____

_____

_____

_____

_____

_____

_____

_____

_____

FATHER'S BLESSING & MOTHER'S BLESSING

Every person ever created has immeasurable value because they were personally and intimately formed by God. No matter the sins, shortcomings, wounding and failures, people are worthy to be loved by God and by man. We all have earthly parents who fail and fall short of the kindness of our Heavenly Father. Even the best parents fail sometimes. It is God's heart that you be blessed by Him and by your earthly father and mother. A father and mother's blessing is tangible and helps people to be secure. Without understanding how deeply loved and accepted we are by Father God, we'll feel and operate under an orphan spirit. Orphans operate in jealousy, rejection, hatred, and shame. God doesn't want us to feel like the jealous elder brother who operated in an orphan spirit in the story of the Prodigal Son related in Luke 15:11-32. God's message to us is the same as the father's, "And he said to him, 'Son, you are always with me, and all that I have is yours.'"

God also wants us to understand that the blessing of the father and mother is important to our well being. It's not just an ethereal concept lacking material substance, rather, the blessing releases tangible effects and is of utmost importance.

In Genesis 27, God shows us the power of the father's blessing. An aging, blind Isaac was set to bless his oldest son, Esau, but his younger son Jacob, through deceit, stole the blessing. Verses 33-35 explain the intentionality and substance of the blessing: "Then Isaac trembled exceedingly, and said, "Who? Where is the one who hunted game and brought it to me? I ate all of it before you came, and I have blessed him---and indeed he shall be blessed." When Esau heard the words of his father, he cried with an exceedingly great and bitter cry, and said to his father, "Bless me---me also, O my father!" But he said, "Your brother came with deceit and has taken away your blessing."

The Lord shows us another example of the blessing through the priestly blessing in Numbers 6:22-27, "And the Lord spoke to Moses, saying: "Speak to Aaron and his sons, saying, 'This is the way you shall bless the children of Israel, say to them: The Lord bless you and keep you; The Lord make His face shine upon you, And be gracious to you; The Lord lift up His countenance upon you, And give you peace,'" "So they shall put My name on the children of Israel, and I will bless them.""

PRAYER ACTIVATION

If you want a blessing from the Lord, I invite you to receive the following and journal below:

"The Lord bless you and keep you. The Lord make His face shine upon you and be gracious to you. The Lord lift up His countenance upon you and give you peace."

_____

_____

_____

_____

_____

_____

_____

_____

_____

_____

_____

_____

_____

_____

_____

_____

As people, our hearts cry out to be blessed by our Heavenly father and by our earthly father and mother. One Father's Day at Bethel Church, Pastor Bill Johnson taught on the father's blessing and then invited anyone to the front to receive a father's blessing from the pastoral team. As he spoke, my heart leapt in me because I knew I needed a father's blessing. Pastor Kris Vallotton prayed over me and released the blessing. I have felt different since that day. I feel settled, loved, respected, wanted, and significant.

PRAYER ACTIVATION

My husband, Joe is a man of integrity and honor. He loves the Lord and is a wonderful husband and father to our three children. If you've never received the blessing of the father before, I invite you to receive the one from Joe below and journal any thoughts:

"Child, you are wanted. Your life is a gift to this world and to those around you. You are significant. You are loved. You are important. I'm so proud of the person you've grown to be. I bless you with peace, with joy, with contentment, with honor, with the ability to make wealth, with integrity, with great earthly relationships, and with the hunger for deep intimacy with your Heavenly Father. I bless you."

_____

_____

_____

_____

_____

_____

_____

_____

_____

_____

_____

_____

_____

_____

PRAYER ACTIVATION

If you want a mother's blessing, I invite you to receive one from me and use the space to journal your thoughts:

"My child, I bless you to know the love of God, to know and be known by family and friends, to grow in character and wisdom, to know the comfort of the Holy Spirit, to grow in the gifts of the Holy Spirit, to grow in confidence and ability. You are loved, you are cherished, you are adored. I'm proud of you. You are doing well in your life. God has many good surprises planned for you. I bless you."

_____

_____

_____

_____

_____

_____

_____

_____

_____

_____

_____

_____

_____

_____

_____

_____

_____

CHAPTER 6

PRACTICAL PROPHETIC

When you're ready to deliver a prophetic word, it is helpful to first understand a few concepts. God created us as a triune person. We are a spirit, we live in a physical body, and we have a soul that comprises our personality, mind, will, and emotions. God can give us a word to help a person in any of these areas. We have to apply solutions that correspond with where the problem lies in a person. If they need spiritual deliverance, ministering to their soul won't bring the answer they need. Pay attention to which area of a person the Holy Spirit wants to minister to. When we minister with the Lord, we are communicating with Him with our spirit, not our mind. Don't think through and analyze with your mind what you're releasing, stay in the flow with Holy Spirit. You may have natural knowledge and wisdom that the Lord will use, but it will be anointed and will release Heaven. If the Lord shows you someone has a digestive problem, ask Him what the key is for that person. Don't assume that the answer for them is apple cider vinegar and probiotics and eating gluten free. Those are valid ways to be healthy naturally but if they need deliverance from a demonic spirit, natural means won't bring the healing. There also might be multiple issues that need addressing. The key is to hear from the Lord, because He knows.

I experienced this when meeting with a new mom friend for coffee. My new friend told me she had been experiencing stomach pain and was nauseous and dizzy. I asked her how long it had been going on. She said since she returned from a mission trip to India four months before. She said that not eating dairy helped minimize her symptoms but she still didn't feel well. I asked the Lord what was going on. He told me she had picked up a parasite in India and to command the parasite to leave her body and to pray for healing for her digestive tract. He also said a demon had attached itself to her on the mission trip and that was causing the dizziness. He said to command it to leave her. I shared with her what I heard the Lord say and asked if I could pray for her. She said yes and I prayed through the keys the Holy Spirit revealed. I saw her again a few months later. She said she got healed that day and hadn't had any symptoms since. That was one example of flowing in the words of wisdom and knowledge. I'll cover those in more detail in the next chapter.

In addition to the multitude of ways God speaks, He can speak through nature, world events, numbers, and other things. Being aware of the Holy Spirit's Presence will allow you to hear from God in unique ways and interpret what He's saying.

People don't usually change by having other people point out their problems. People change when the supernatural grace to change is extended to them. A prophetic word by its very nature carries the grace to accomplish the word. Frequently, the prophetic word initiates a process toward growth and change and not instantaneous deliverance. God is interested in our character growth and our ability to retain the freedom He gives us. I heard Prophet Dick Mills share this concept brilliantly. At the time he preached at Bethel Church in Redding, he was in his mid 80s. He shared that God had just delivered him in a major way that year and he told God it would have been helpful to him (and his wife!) if God hadn't waited till he was in his 80s to accomplish it for him. God replied that He hadn't waited and that He had worked as quickly as possible in his life. God explained that before He could do that, He had to do this, and before He could do this, He had to do this other thing and before that He had to do another thing. God had been working diligently to bring Dick Mills to maturity and it was a lifelong process. God works with each of us in that manner. We can pursue God and trust His process with us when we understand this concept. We can also understand that this is the manner in which people change and grow. There are some suddenlies and supernatural deliverances that move us rapidly forward but in between is a lot of process time. Praying for ourselves and others is a main component for helping all of us grow.

PRAYER ACTIVATION

Journal the timeline of encounters you've had with the Lord that has brought about change in your character and freedom for you. Ask the Lord to highlight His inner workings in your heart to build your faith in your journey with Him. Ask Him what He's currently doing in your life.

_____

_____

_____

_____

_____

_____

_____

_____

_____

_____

_____

_____

_____

_____

THE SEER REALM

Seeing the help we have in the seer realm can boost our faith in partnering to bring Heaven to earth. Some of the following the Lord has shown me personally and some He has shown other seers.

When believers extend their hands to pray for people, it's a literal release of supernatural, not symbolic. Multi colored light rays extend powerfully from each hand toward the person receiving prayer. It looks like something you'd see in a super hero movie. The colors of light vary in intensity and color, depending upon what is being released. Every time we pray, God responds.

There is a portal to Heaven over every married couple's bed. This allows the couple to be connected to God in their intimacy with each other and in their sleep. Heaven honors covenant. I've been asked if there is a portal over the beds of single people and I don't know because I haven't seen it. However, God wants relationship with each of us so asking Him for one over our children and ourselves is an invitation He won't refuse. I've seen a waterfall in my living room that releases revelation and angelic activity. I also see and feel an angel by the chair I sit in. Whenever I sit there, I connect to the Lord and hear from Him more quickly because of the angel that is stationed there.

People have 1-2 guardian angels stationed with them for their lifetime. We will also have more angels in our houses and for specific kingdom assignments. The Lord showed me my angels one day as I was in prayer. One of them is very tall and extremely skinny, only a few inches wide in profile. I was honestly quite shocked at his appearance. I asked why he was so thin. The angel responded to me and said it is because I put him in really tight spots. That still makes me chuckle. My other angel is normal height and a bit rotund. He's also quite funny. By nature, I'm not funny. The Lord told me that the angel will say funny things and I'll repeat what he says and get a laugh from people.

One of my seer friends recounts a time when she wasn't walking with the Lord. She still could see her angels and was familiar with their presence and protection. One night as she was being inappropriate with a boyfriend, she saw her angels turn around. They didn't leave her but they couldn't look upon sin. Seeing her angels' response made her realize that she was grieving the heart of God with her actions.

There is a spot on the upper back of people, just above the left shoulder blade that is a prophetic spot. When prophetic people are flowing with declarations and prayer properly, that spot will feel fine. When they are a little backed up and need to declare what Heaven is saying, that spot will get tight and painful. It's not a natural cause and won't be healed through massage or chiropractic care. It's a spiritual cause that requires a spiritual cure of prayer. Praying in tongues frequently keeps prophetic people healthy. God will also show us in dreams when we are not able to speak that we need to pray and declare more.

Through the years as I've prayed for people, the Lord would tell me which hand to use. He was very specific. When I inquired what the difference was, He showed me that my left hand carries healing and my right hand carries authority. (For deliverance to occur, authority is required). Genesis 48 tells the interesting account of Jacob blessing Joseph's sons Manasseh and Ephraim. Jacob crossed his hands over in the blessing in order to lay his right hand on the younger son, Ephraim. Joseph tried to correct Jacob in order for him to release his blessing from his right hand on the oldest son. Jacob replied that the youngest son would indeed be greater than the firstborn.

When a person is wounded and feels deep insecurity, it often lodges in a person's lower abdomen area. It can cause an aching type pain and physical problems to manifest in female organs, the bladder, lower digestive tract and the appendix. After a particularly hard season, I had a constant dull ache in my lower abdomen, as well as a pervasive feeling of insecurity. Joe and I were praying one night and I saw the Lord put His hand on both Joe's and my lower abdomens and release healing. The next time we prayed together, the Lord again put His hand of healing on our lower abdomens. The ache in my body and my heart was gone after that and I felt secure in His love and our circumstances.

God loves for the angels to help in bringing the power of prayer to pass. After we moved to Raleigh, there was a battle in the spirit over my seer authority. It took almost 18 months for me to get traction and then God rewarded me with an increase. During the battle, it was like a bronze ceiling over my head. When I traveled out of state, I could hear/see perfectly. In Raleigh, I experienced trouble with dreams, had a persistent eye infection for months, and was frustrated. One of my prophetic daughters also experienced the same trouble seeing. At the end of the battle as I got victory, God told me to declare that we had authority to see. He also had a prophet pray for me to see in the spirit. A few nights after my daughter and I made the declaration that we could see, I woke up because an orange angel was standing at the foot of my bed. He directed my attention to a small blue screen by the wall that he had brought with him. As I looked at it, the screen came over to me. When it was directly in front of me, it released a spray of blue light/mist into my right eye. The angel told me that I now had authority to see and disappeared into the night. Everything shifted after that encounter.

PRAYER ACTIVATION

If you realize that you're doing something in your life that grieves the Lord's heart, take a moment to repent. Ask Jesus to forgive you and set you free from any wounds or lies or anything demonic associated with your actions. If you related to my recounting my healing of insecurity, place your hand on your lower abdomen and ask the Lord to heal you of insecurity. Journal what the Lord shows you here.

_____

_____

_____

_____

_____

_____

_____

_____

_____

_____

_____

PRAYER ACTIVATION

Record any keys the Lord has shown you personally in the seer realm. Journal and share with a friend any insights you have.

_____

_____

_____

_____

_____

_____

_____

_____

_____

_____

_____

_____

THE PROCESS OF REVELATION/INTERPRETATION/APPLICATION

When the Lord gives you revelation from Heaven, the process is not complete until you also receive the interpretation and the application. Pictures almost always need an interpretation from the Lord for them to be helpful. And then hearing from the Lord timing and steps for application round out the prophetic word process.

The types of words you'll receive from God will include who He is, the person's unique identity, purpose, inner healing, deliverance, direction, and others. You'll receive the word through one of the four primary ways of knowing, hearing, seeing, and feeling. You'll often flow back and forth between the ways God speaks effortlessly. After you get the word, ask

God for the interpretation and for more about it. He loves the interactive dialogue with us as we prophesy. Investigative questions such as who, what, why, where, when, and how are helpful. This part of the process is done before you ever open your mouth to speak the word. Deliver what you've gotten thus far and ask God another investigative question. Continue this process until you don't get anything further from the Lord about the initial word. If the word is anointed and it appears to be doing a work in the person's heart, wait. If not, move on. Ask the Lord for another word for them. Remember to get the interpretation. It may not be relevant to share the picture you got with them. Don't dance around by describing in minute detail the word; don't bore your person. Taking five minutes to describe one word doesn't add more value. Getting five distinct words for them in five minutes does. The person and the Holy Spirit have a role in unpacking prophecy. If you're not getting more revelation, move on to another word. Being direct and specific gives the person a deeper impact and ability to understand and recall the word. When you're ministering with a group and it gets silent, make sure you're not moving onto another word or interrupting any healing God is doing in the person. Learn to flow with what Holy Spirit is doing.

It is both the believer's job and the person receiving the word's job to witness to the word that is prophesied. Especially as a person is learning to prophesy, part of the word will be correct, and part may not be. They may get the revelation correct but miss the application or timing. As the person progresses in maturity, a larger percentage will be accurate. It's just part of the learning process. If you receive a word but you have trouble sorting out what is correct and what isn't, throw it out and ask the Lord to give it to you again or ask Him to show you personally. If you're a feeler, an accurate word will feel peaceful and warm in your upper stomach/diaphragm area. An incorrect word will feel like a "thud" in that same area. People who "know" will sense it's right or wrong. If you don't function with discernment, you'll have to hear or see directly from the Lord about words. Just because your soul doesn't like a word, doesn't make it wrong. It is your job to steward the words the Lord gives you. I'll discuss more about stewarding words in chapter 12.

CHAPTER 7

REVELATORY GIFTS

The Holy Spirit works with us through the revelatory gifts of the word of knowledge, word of wisdom and discerning of spirits.

These gifts of the Holy Spirit are mentioned in 1 Corinthians 12:7-11, "But the manifestation of the Spirit is given to each one for the profit of all: for to one is given the word of wisdom through the Spirit, to another the word of knowledge through the same Spirit, to another faith by the same Spirit, to another gifts of healings by the same Spirit, to another working of miracles, to another prophecy, to another discerning of spirits, to another different kinds of tongues, to another the interpretation of tongues. But one and the same Spirit works all these things, distributing to each one individually as He wills."

WORD OF KNOWLEDGE

God can show us details about people that we couldn't possibly know through a word of knowledge. The purpose of the knowledge is to get their attention, to let them know they are deeply loved and known by the Father. That opens their heart to receive a prophetic word, salvation, healing, or instruction. Functioning with words of knowledge is not meant to draw attention to the person giving the word, but to Jesus and to give Him glory. Also, a word of knowledge needs to be followed by more of the prophetic to accomplish what God wants to say to people. Prophet Shawn Bolz of Expression 58 in Los Angeles, California has grown immeasurably in recent years in his revelatory gift. He's called out addresses, phone numbers, birth dates, anniversary dates publicly that show how intimately God sees people. He follows that up with specific prophetic words. It's wonderful to watch people get touched and loved on by Shawn and by God. Shawn is forerunning what we as the Body of Christ should carry. No one would ever be deceived by the occult if the Church carried prophetic revelation to that degree. It's an invitation to you and to me to grow and steward our prophetic gifting. I encourage you to watch some of Shawn's prophesying on YouTube and to ask God for an increase in your own gifting.

Another way the word of knowledge functions is as a diagnosis. As you're ministering to a person, you may get a pain in your body that is not yours but is a clue that God wants to bring healing in that area. As you pray for that person because of the word of knowledge, they will get healed. This also functions similarly for ministering to crowds.

WORD OF WISDOM

Whereas words of knowledge are diagnoses, words of wisdom are solutions or treatment plans. They are not intuitive or something you think through with your natural mind, rather they are keys that come directly from the Holy Spirit. Medical doctors who partner with God see more correct diagnoses and healings through words of knowledge and wisdom. The example I gave in a previous chapter about praying for the mom whose stomach hurt and was nauseous and dizzy was an example of partnering with God with words of knowledge and wisdom. The word of knowledge was the diagnosis that the pain came from a parasite and the nausea and dizziness came from a demonic spirit. The word of wisdom was the treatment plan of praying for healing for the stomach and deliverance for the demonic spirit. God brought the key for healing and she was instantly healed and delivered after months of suffering.

Jesus gave us the mandate to disciple nations and to bring the culture of Heaven to earth. We can partner with Him in the realms of society to bring the Kingdom. Christian business people should partner with words of wisdom to bring financial success to companies. God has the perfect strategy for success in every situation. Christians who are proficient in the revelatory gifts will be highlighted and promoted. Governments need God's timing and solutions for the myriad of problems the world faces. Josephs, Daniels, Davids and Solomons are being raised up during this time to bring wisdom to the world.

DISCERNING OF SPIRITS

Discerning of spirits is a supernatural gifting to perceive what God's Spirit, man's spirit, angelic spirits and demonic spirits are doing. God often uses this revelatory gift in dreams where He shows solutions, problems and root issues and how to partner with Him in navigating successful living. People who are feelers function strongly in this gifting. Calibrating and maturity are important and can be derailed through rejection and paranoia. Growing in wisdom in the use of discerning of spirits requires help from more mature believers. When children have this gift, it's important to help them understand what they're sensing is real, no matter how things seem on the surface. Often, the purpose for this gifting is intercession to bring things into alignment with God's purposes. Business people who function in this gifting can avoid pitfalls and have awareness on how to choose healthy business partners and deals.

PRAYER ACTIVATION

I release an impartation to activate you in the words of knowledge and wisdom and discerning of spirits in your walk with Him. Journal examples of how these are already operating in your life. Ask the Lord for practice opportunities in the coming weeks.

_____

_____

_____

CHAPTER 8

WHO'S WHO IN THE PROPHETIC

PROPHETIC PEOPLE

The gift of prophesying is for all believers. It is a gift from the Holy Spirit that we can all be activated in, practice and grow in.

The Apostle Paul encourages us in 1 Corinthians 14:1-5 to "Pursue love, and desire spiritual gifts, but especially that you may prophesy. For he who speaks in a tongue does not speak to men but to God, for no one understands him; however, in the spirit he speaks mysteries. But he who prophesies speaks edification and exhortation and comfort to men. He who speaks in a tongue edifies himself, but he who prophesies edifies the church. I wish you all spoke with tongues, but even more that you prophesied; for he who prophesies is greater than he who speaks with tongues, unless indeed he interprets, that the church may receive edification."

Paul makes clear that prophecy edifies, exhorts and comforts and is important for the health of the church. He goes on to reveal in 1 Corinthians 14:24-25 about the power of prophecy for unbelievers. "But if all prophesy, and an unbeliever or an uninformed person comes in, he is convinced by all, he is convicted by all. And thus the secrets of his heart are revealed; and so, falling down on his face, he will worship God and report that God is truly among you."

We owe the world an encounter with God and prophecy is a bridge for people to experience Him, in all His wonder. When Paul mentions that the secrets of the heart are revealed through prophecy, he is not talking about secret sin. He is referring to the depths of who a person is created to be. We've all fallen short of the glory of God (Romans 3:23) and when people are exposed to the glory they were called to carry to bring honor to God, it causes them to worship and turn to God. That's a duty that we have as God's ambassadors here on this earth.

Prophesying does not have to be dramatic to be profound. It's as simple as asking God for a prophetic word for a co-worker, or the local coffee barista or the server at lunch. A prophetic word by nature is anointed with the presence of the Holy Spirit. Even unbelievers can sense the difference between a prophetic word and a friendly, encouraging word. Remember, even though prophetic words are encouraging and edifying, it doesn't mean a word that is encouraging and edifying is prophetic. A word is prophetic if it originates from the Trinity.

PROPHETIC CULTURE

Prophetic people are called to reveal the heart of the Father, to reveal love. They are to encourage, edify, comfort, build-up and to call out the gold in people's lives. They are not to correct with the prophetic, nor call out sin. They call out people's specific identity and calling and they release kisses from a good God.

Typical guidelines for a prophetic community include not calling out "Mates, Dates, or Babies" as a protection for the hearts of those they are prophesying over. We don't want to cause harm by prophesying something that they should be hearing directly from God or through counsel with their pastor.

I have a high value for learning to hear timing and seasons from God, which I'll cover in chapter 10. For whatever reason, timing takes a lot of practice to become accurate in. Because releasing timing requires practice, a disclaimer should always be included when prophesying timing.

I had the opportunity to prophesy over a conservative group of high school students who had never experienced prophecy before. They were so hungry to hear what the Lord thought of them and were hungry to hear destiny. Over the previous few months, I had noticed one young man was pretty forward with the young ladies and made them uneasy with his intentions. As I asked the Lord for a word for him, God showed me that he designed him to be a lover. That made sense to me, although I could see how his actions made those around him uncomfortable. I told the young man that God designed him to be a lover. I then gave him wisdom that he needed to wait to walk in that with a woman until he was married and that he would be a very special husband to a fortunate woman. He beamed and held his head high as I spoke his God given identity to him. A few months later his mom introduced herself to me and thanked me for what I had spoken to her son. She said he had changed considerably toward his siblings and one night at dinner she complimented him on his kindness to his siblings. His response to her was, "Of course, I'm kind. I'm a lover."

PROPHETIC WORSHIPPERS

Worship leaders and worshippers in the congregation are called to sense what the Lord is doing and respond in kind to bring Heaven to earth. Prophetic worshippers create open heavens for the angels to enter an area. They usher in more of the presence of the Lord. They may also prophesy through song as they hear the word of the Lord. The anointing on a worship leader's life is directly related to their intimacy with the Lord. It doesn't correspond to their musical talent; it parallels their individual relationship. They can only take a congregation in worship where they go in individual intimacy.

PROPHETIC INTERCESSORS

Intercession that is powerful and effective involves sensing what the Lord is doing and making the appropriate declarations. The Lord will give intercessors keys to solve problems and bring heaven to earth. Learning the ways that God communicates is helpful both for prophesying and for powerful intercession.

PRAYER ACTIVATION

I release to you an impartation for an increase in your prophetic gifting and for courage and opportunities to share. Remember, the Nabi' flow prophetic is the fastest way to prophesy when time is short. Journal any questions you have for God and record any testimonies you have here to stir up your faith for more.

_____

_____

_____

_____

_____

_____

_____

_____

_____

_____

_____

_____

_____

_____

OFFICE OF THE PROPHET

The office of the prophet is one of the 5-fold governmental offices given by Christ.

The 5-fold is kingdom government for the equipping of the saints as described in Ephesians 4:11-13, "And He Himself gave some to be apostles, some prophets, some evangelists, and some pastors and teachers, for the equipping of the saints for the work of ministry, for the edifying of the body of Christ, till we all come to the unity of the faith and of the knowledge of the Son of God, to a perfect man, to the measure of the stature of the fullness of Christ."

Being called to an office is a gift from Christ and He is the One who already decided whom He has called. Man doesn't choose or appoint those in 5-fold offices. Christ calls people at birth, at salvation, at making Jesus Lord, at the Baptism of the Holy Spirit, or another time. Some people are called and yet never walk in their call. Graham Cooke writes that it takes thirteen years for a prophet to be set in the office and it happens when they are recognized both by God and by man. Prior to being set in the office, they are in a preparation time where they are learning to function in their gifts and building character and wisdom. God likes to tell prophets Himself that He has chosen them to lead, however, some learn through a prophetic word. In that case, it often comes as a confirmation to the stirring in their hearts.

The size of the prophetic gift does not make one a prophet or not make one a prophet. There will be prophetic people with bigger gifts than some prophets. Being able to prophesy does not make one a prophet. Being able to prophesy is a gift given from the Holy Spirit for the purpose of edification, exhortation and comfort. The office of the prophet is a gift given by Christ for equipping the saints. The purpose of prophets is many fold. They are called to equip, intercede, minister to God, make declarations, help people transition, lead people to closer relationship with God, be a voice, write. Every prophet is an intercessor by design/call. Not every intercessor is a prophet.

Prophets are often very black and white in their perspectives and personalities. God designed them that way, but also works with them to soften their edges so that their voices are better received. Prophet Arthur Burk has written extensively on the strengths and weaknesses of prophets. According to Arthur, strengths of prophets include: strong leadership, highly adaptable, ideologically driven, strong national identity, fiercely competitive, willingness to do newness, willingness to sacrifice deeply, ability to dream and see beyond the horizon, walk in faith, belief in the impossible. They are rebuilders, problem solvers, passionate, generous, intense, articulate, creative, intuitive and they see the future and how it is supposed to look.

Prophets also carry significant weaknesses that need to be modified by the Lord: they are never satisfied, they always fine tune and fix. They will defend ideas at the expense of relationship. Justice vs love. They can be intense, moody, judgmental, extreme. Greed, power, and corruption can result when the fear of the Lord is not present in their lives.

Prophets have the ability to release a transition grace to people at all stages of life. They can declare a word that helps people get pregnant, move, transfer jobs, pass to Heaven, and any other transition in life. The grace is released when they speak the word. If they don't speak it, it may not happen. They have the ability to create the future by their declaration. With wisdom, if they clearly hear the Lord tell them to prophesy a future baby or a specific date, they need to speak it and release the grace for the event to happen.

When my mom was dying, she spent 4 weeks in the ICU before she passed. A few weeks before she died, the Lord told me that He needed me to not just be a daughter during this time but also a prophet to help her transition. He told me to listen for Him to tell me when to make a declaration that it was time for her to pass to Heaven. Two days before she died, I heard Him say it was time so I made the declaration. There were some pretty difficult family dynamics surrounding her death that precipitated the need for help in her transition. I also had a dream during the month that she was in a coma where she told me to tell my Father that she was being tormented and needed help. I took authority over her and bound any demonics that were tormenting her and released angelic protection for her.

OVERCOMING FOR PROPHETS

Somehow the enemy knows the call on peoples' lives and tries to stop them. Walking in righteousness in family lines helps prophets in the call on their lives. All prophets have to be free from fear, control, fear of man, sexual sin, religious spirits, sickness, death, physical pain, and financial sin to operate fully in their anointing. The enemy tries to exploit each of these areas in a prophet's life to nullify their call. Families who have generations who gain freedom in these areas pass the freedom on to the prophets in their generation. First generation Christians who are prophets spend more time in their preparation seasons overcoming in these areas.

PRAYER ACTIVATION

Ask the Lord to show you your specific life call. Ask Him if you are called to a 5- fold office in the Body and if so, which one. Ask Him to confirm whatever He shows you. Journal your thoughts here.

_____

_____

_____

_____

_____

_____

_____

_____

CHAPTER 9

POWER IN CREATING THE FUTURE

FORETELLING

Foretelling is the ability to see the future. We can use our prophetic gift to see what the future holds in peoples' lives. What we are seeing is what God has planned and what the angels are working to accomplish. We can add our amen to God's plan by declaring it in a prophetic word. This gives people confidence in their future and gives them a word to war with against anything coming against that future. God's will does not always happen, even though He is sovereign, because of free will and enemy interference. God needs our cooperation through prayer and action; foretelling the future through a prophetic word is one way we partner with Him.

We can also potentially see the enemy's plans through foretelling. When we see something that has the mark of the enemy on it that is to kill, steal or destroy, we can cancel those plans through prayer, intercession and prophetic declaration. We don't want to agree with the negative plan, so we use our prophetic ability to cancel the assignment. If you see something negative, don't speak it over the person. The purpose of seeing it is for intercession on their behalf. It is important not to release fear over a person by speaking a negative prophetic word. If you see it, you have the authority to take care of it. Ask God what He wants to release instead. He has hope and a future for every person. Declare life over them and their future.

PRAYER ACTIVATION

Record examples of foretelling you've experienced in both receiving and giving prophetic words.

_____

_____

_____

_____

_____

_____

_____

_____

_____

_____

FORTHTELLING

Forthtelling is the ability to create the future by declaration. At creation, God spoke the world into existence. As His children, we also have the ability to create with our words. Our words are important. Death and life are in the power of the tongue. Be sure you are speaking life and blessing, not death and cursing. Be careful to hear the will of God in a situation and not be presumptive in declarations.

People can also get a bump in the speed of their process when a prophet with a strong anointing declares something for them. This works best when the prophet hears the word directly from the Lord rather than being asked to declare something over a person.

We experienced the acceleration a prophet provides to help in transition when God called us to move to Redding. Sometime during the two year process it took for us to move to California, He told us to go to Texas. My husband and I went to Texas for a weekend and visited four churches. We didn't know why God wanted us to go but we were diligent to seek it out. At the 4th church service, Prophet Chuck Pierce was in the congregation. We arrived late because we had already attended another church service that morning. We stood in the back during worship. We were worshipping with our eyes closed when suddenly Chuck Pierce tapped us on the shoulder. He proceeded to prophesy over us and declare things over our future. Later, the Lord told me that Chuck's anointing to shift things into place saved us five years of walking it out ourselves. Thank you Lord!

PRAYER ACTIVATION

Journal any experiences you've had with forthtelling. Ask the Lord to activate this in your walk with Him.

_____

_____

_____

_____

_____

_____

_____

_____

_____

_____

_____

_____

_____

_____

FALSE PROPHETS

False prophets are not prophets or prophetic people who get a prophetic word wrong. The stoning of prophets in the Old Testament for inaccurate words was because during that dispensation in history only the prophets and kings could hear from the Lord. Therefore, any deception on their part was devastating to the people, and required strong consequences. If you're prophesying and you later realize your word was inaccurate, take responsibility and apologize for it but don't worry about being stoned for it.

False prophets are prophets who through rebellion, wounding and deception are now partnering with an antichrist spirit. They are not in relationship with the Body of Christ, they release fear, and don't operate in love. They justify their rejection because they believe they are always right and are flawless in hearing from the Lord. They often have been wounded by spiritual leadership. They can be redeemed but need to be in covenant relationship with the Body of Christ and need to submit to spiritual authority and protocol. The revelation that we are important and get our identity from being children of God and not from our gifts or what we do is central to the healing of false prophets.

DIVINATION/FLATTERY

Divination is the use of the prophetic to flatter or manipulate. It is an intentional use of giving a person a directive or corrective or flattering word that is from the person but is represented as a prophetic word. The key here is that the person knows that it is his or her opinion but presents it as from the Lord.

Kim Clement writes about a bad experience with receiving a divination word. A small group of people prophesied that he would have a home in Egypt and a few other nice things. Kim didn't witness to the word, but was intrigued by having a large home in the Middle East. Shortly after that word, Kim experienced major back pain and had a few surgeries that didn't relieve the pain. As he prayed and asked the Lord why his back wasn't being healed, the Lord reminded him of the word he received about an Egyptian home. God told him it was a word of flattery and not a prophetic word from Him. He told him to cancel the word. As Kim did, his back was healed.

I, too, experienced receiving a corrective divination word from a woman at church years ago. I had been learning about the spiritual realm and was having God and angelic encounters, as well as some demonic encounters. It was new to me, and I was thrown into them after receiving the Baptism of the Holy Spirit. The encounters scared a woman I knew and she told me that God was saying to back off and that my spiritual experiences were not of Him and she gave me a Scripture to back it up. I knew they were of God, except for the demonic ones, but I wanted to be teachable so I received the word. Very soon after that word, a cloud of depression and hopelessness came over me. Six months later, God told me to buy Kim Clement's book, "Secrets of the Prophetic". As I read his account of his back pain caused by divination and subsequent healing, the Lord told me that the hopelessness and depression I was experiencing was because of my having received the corrective divination word. I repented and cancelled the word. As soon as I did, the entire house brightened up and I felt the cloud lift.

In cases of divination, you'll know the word is wrong. If the word is confusing to you because it is a mixture of correct, incorrect or your soul doesn't like it, it doesn't mean that divination has occurred. The way to handle it when you receive a word that you're not sure about is to pray that the word is filtered through the Holy Spirit and that anything that is not of Him would drop off. Then ask Him to highlight to you any part that is from Him and what you should steward. If you're still not sure, flush the word and ask God to give it to you again if it is from Him. We want to have tender hearts toward the Lord and say yes to anything He wants for our lives so we don't want to discount anything that is of Him.

PRAYER ACTIVATION

Ask the Lord to purify your prophetic flow and cancel any words that originated in divination or flattery.

_____

_____

_____

_____

_____

_____

_____

_____

_____

_____

WITCHCRAFT

Witchcraft is the deliberate use of spiritual power to manipulate and control. The demonic principality Jezebel is behind witchcraft. Discernment of witchcraft is often experienced through dizziness. Witchcraft may be floating around a city trying to get a stronghold or it may be trying to hurt an individual or get an individual's agreement. It's important when we discern witchcraft that we don't get paranoid and assume that where we felt it is in agreement with it. Believe what is lovely, and of good report. Witchcraft also tries to divide and break up covenant. Just ask the Lord how to respond with wisdom. Release self-control and the Lord's plan where you discern it. The Lord's kingdom is never meant to be manipulated or controlled. Operating in spiritual gifts is a privilege from the Lord and not to be used for personal gain or manipulation. The Lord is trustworthy and has good plans for you and for me. We are not to take control. Lucifer tried to seize control from God.

If I sense a person I'm in relationship with struggles with control, I pray that all of our interactions filter through the Cross of Jesus. That keeps that control spirit from operating at me, yet helps me to enjoy the friendship. We are all in the process of getting free from demonic influences and growing in character, so we need to have grace for one another. However, if people struggle with control, they should not be put in a leadership position until they are free from it so they don't hurt other people.

PRAYER ACTIVATION

If need be, repent from any attempts at partnering with a witchcraft spirit to control situations or other people. Ask the Lord to deliver you from a witchcraft spirit. Commit to trusting the Lord in your life. Journal any thoughts here.

_____

_____

_____

_____

_____

_____

_____

_____

_____

_____

_____

_____

Annie Blouin

CHAPTER 10

ISSACHAR ANOINTING/SEASONS

Ecclesiastes 3:1-8, "There is a time for everything, and a season for every activity under the heavens: a time to be born and a time to die, a time to plant and a time to uproot, a time to kill and a time to heal, a time to tear down and a time to build, a time to weep and a time to laugh, a time to mourn and a time to dance, a time to scatter stones and a time to gather them, a time to embrace and a time to refrain from embracing, a time to search and a time to give up, a time to keep and a time to throw away, a time to tear and a time to mend, a time to be silent and a time to speak, a time to love and a time to hate, a time for war and a time for peace."

Because there are different seasons all around us, we need to hear from the Lord what season we are in on a regular basis so we can position ourselves correctly in partnering with Him. We can pursue carrying the anointing to know seasons like the sons of Issachar in Israel.

1 Chronicles 12:32 NIV, "From the tribe of Issachar, there were 200 leaders of the tribe with their relatives. All these men understood the signs of the times and knew the best course for Israel to take."

Understanding times and seasons is another part of the seer dimension. The seer anointing is not just to see visions, but it's also to have understanding of how things look in the spirit: seeing what structures exist or what need to exist or what need to be removed. For instance, in healing, looking into the seer realm for the root of the problem (whether it's in the spirit, soul, or body) and then discerning the solution within each realm.

Spirit- Deliverance, God Encounter, Identity Words

Soul- Inner Healing, Replacing Lies with Truth, Communication Tools, Healing From Co-Dependency

Body- Supernatural Healing, Medical Field Healing, Natural/Nutritional Healing

For example, I prayed for a young mom with a breast tumor who came into the Bethel Healing Rooms. The tumor was large. She could feel it protrude into her upper arm. I asked God how He wanted to heal the woman. I was prompted to lead her on an encounter in Heaven with Father God. She quickly saw herself sitting on Papa's lap and I had her ask God if He would protect her. She heard Him say He would. At that revelation, she was delivered from fear and the tumor instantly dissolved. She burst into tears at experiencing God's healing and deliverance. The entire miracle took place in under two minutes. The fear was replaced with the truth of God's protection and the lie and the fruit of the lie had to leave her body. The root of that tumor was spiritual and not in the soul or the body and had to be dealt with in the spirit for the miracle to occur. And by exposing the lie, she would retain her healing.

Understanding times and seasons can help us partner well with God. We are currently in a time of Kingdom building and expansion on the earth, not an end times shaking time. Heaven is directing resources to believers for expansion.

I believe there are current day Issachar prophets who carry a strong anointing for discerning the corporate times. Doug Addison is one. I also believe that all believers are called to carry their own understanding for their personal lives and individual calling. There are very practical applications for the season anointing: timing on buying houses, jobs, children, aging parents, business plans, government administration, governing decisions, inventions, and lots of others.

My husband and I were in a very challenging financial season a few years ago. We have a wise friend who had been through his own financial wilderness years earlier and is now quite prosperous. He told us that he wouldn't help us financially, because it would only prolong our season. That gave me comfort that he could see our season clearly and that it would indeed end.

There are seasons released from Heaven that carry the anointing to accomplish what the season holds. There was an eighteen-month period while we lived in Redding where God was focused on helping peoples' souls and marriages heal. It was an intense time but the people who understood the Divine season and partnered with it saw great breakthrough. When that window passed, it was harder to get marital traction until it came back around again a few years later.

Pay attention to what the corporate anointing is seasonally and position yourself accordingly. You can also have your own individual seasons; no matter what else is going on corporately. You can also have seasons within seasons. The anointing eases the process.

Churches have unique seasons and all churches have unique callings. The mandate of individual churches is their assignment from God. Churches can be assigned to highlight certain parts of the Gospel and can be appointed to raise different age believers. Some churches are similar to elementary schools, some like junior high or high schools, and some are for advanced Christianity. Recognize that this is God's prerogative and strategy. No one church can be all things to all people. Don't judge and just be where God has called you.

In April 2014, I heard God say that Bethel Church in Redding was undergoing a "Changing of the Guard". I knew that meant there would be a major personnel change. Over the course of the next five months, almost all of the administrative staff changed and many faithful mature people moved on to other promotions and assignments. More words came out that Bethel was releasing mature Oaks to be planted in other locations.

My journey into knowing and loving seasons began in Redding. My seer gift sees far into the future and learning to be content in the present has been a process for me. In order to help me, God told me to buy a decorative plaque that says "Love in the present". During our challenging financial season, I asked God for money to pay our bills. He told me that wasn't what He was doing in us right then, rather, He was working on restoring our extended family relationships. In my desperation, I told Him that I didn't care about that, that I just wanted money. That impassioned plea didn't change His mind or my season. I learned that knowing my season was helpful for me to partner with God better to be patient in the present. I also learned the key to life is the realization that true wealth is the fact that God walks with you in every circumstance. No matter what else happens, good or bad, He is the true prize.

I always ask God what He is doing corporately and in our family at Rosh Hashanah each year. The Jewish New Year is still God's time clock and begins sometime in September or October each year. I also ask Him again for the January 1st New Year for anything else He is doing in the country or world or our city. I receive personal words from Him for my year that I partner with and track. I love season words and often prophesy people's seasons to them. I encourage everyone to learn to partner with God in this manner.

When people receive a prophetic word, it almost always initiates a process. The word is the seed that grows over time until it becomes mature. Peering into the seer realm through the lens of seasons gives us construct for what actions to take to be sure that we receive a good harvest and don't abort our word.

What does it look like practically to partner with knowing our seasons? In my experience, God gives me seasons thus far that are 4-7 months long and have a theme. Some are passive seasons on my part where He is doing the work and some are very active on my part. I've actively tracked seasons now for the past three years. I ask God a few days before the season changes for what the next season is. I am very purposeful to not think through what I think it may be. I just wait to hear. And He always tells me, because He enjoys seasons as much as I do.

Listed here are the themes and timing of each season of mine for the past three years.

<u>July-November 2013.</u>   Authority over Lack.

This was a major warfare season that was so difficult, I absolutely needed to know when it ended so that I could persevere.

<u>December 2013-April 2014.</u>   Heart Healing.

Not surprising after the previous season. It felt a lot like being in the intensive care unit.

<u>May-August 2014.</u>   Joshua 1:11, Prepare to cross the Jordan.

Hearing this season word, as well as Him telling me we would live in the apartment we had just rented for six months, made me suspect we were moving cross country in September. I've learned with God, though, not to assume. Practical steps I took during these months was to clear out closets, have garage sales, spend a lot of time with friends, and finish my daughter's baby scrapbook.

<u>September-December 2014.</u>   Establishment.

We moved to Raleigh, NC September 2nd and spent the next 4 months getting settled both naturally and spiritually. Anytime we've moved, it takes some time to settle in the land. The demonic in the new area doesn't like what we bring and has to be put under our authority, so there was a bit of small warfare during this time. Our new pastor, Duncan Smith, helped this process tremendously because the first time he met us, he prayed and commanded the land and the business community to welcome us. He welcomed us in to his land spiritually and he eased our transition.

<u>January-April 2015.</u>   Understanding Spiritual Structures.

This was a time where God spoke to me and gave me a few dreams to show me what things looked like in the spirit that would impact the natural realm. Other than spending time with God as usual, it was a passive season on my part.

<u>May-October 2015.</u>   Promised Land.

Notice that this season was not back to back with the Joshua 1:11 season the fall before? Can't assume anything, have to hear it from God. This season was happy with some squirmishes in receiving God's bounty. My husband got a significant raise during this time, as well as some other fun things for our family.

<u>November 2015-April 2016.</u>   Joy.

This was a season where God was establishing joy in me as a primary state. It was the culmination of nearly a decade long process. The season was uncomfortable, like being pregnant, but I was thankful for what it was building in me.

<u>May-November 2016.</u>   Writing.

Very active season on my part. I'm writing this prophetic manual and working on two other book projects. I had heard from the Lord at Rosh Hashanah that 2016 was a time of writing for me but I didn't get any traction in the first few months of the year. I was thankful to hear that there was an actual writing season dispensation for the year.

I hope that I've given you a taste for loving seasons and a hunger for pursuing relationship with God in your own seasons. I really believe the world needs what we carry as the Body of Christ.

PRAYER ACTIVATION

I impart what I carry in loving, carrying, and understanding the Issachar anointing. Receive it and be faithful in practicing. Take the included space to ask God what your current season theme is and when it started and when it ends. With this lens in mind, identify the previous few seasons and ask God what His overall purpose for you in this time is.

CHAPTER 11

DREAM INTERPRETATION

I have studied dream interpretation extensively and have also learned through my own experiences with God. This chapter will be a combination of my own revelation, as well as revelation from John Paul Jackson, Barbie Breathitt, James Goll and others. John Paul Jackson became an expert in dream interpretation and like Scripture exhorts, studied to show himself approved. If you want to grow deeper, I recommend John Paul's materials on dream interpretation.

Throughout Scripture, dreams are a primary way God speaks to His people.

Genesis 37:5-11 details the account of Joseph's dreams about being great and his family serving him. His dreams gave Joseph courage as he endured being thrown into a pit, sold into slavery, and locked in prison. The dreams of the promise from God forged his identity even through the process.

Isaiah 29:5 explains in the context of a disobedient Israel how we are all nourished through God dreams, "It shall even be as when a hungry man dreams, and look – he eats; or as when a thirsty man dreams, and look – he drinks."

God gave very specific directions to Joseph, father of Jesus in dreams. Matthew 2:13 tells us of one such occasion, "Now when they had departed, behold, an angel of the Lord appeared to Joseph in a dream, saying, 'Arise, take the young Child and His mother, flee to Egypt, and stay there until I bring you word; for Herod will seek the young Child to destroy Him.'"

God also gives dreams to unbelievers for governing purposes. Some dreams they can interpret themselves, like Pilate's wife in Matthew 27:19, "While he (Jesus) was sitting on the judgment seat, Pilate's wife sent to Pilate and said, 'Have nothing to do with that just Man, for I have suffered many things today in a dream because of Him.'"

Others in leadership have dreams they need help interpreting. Jacob's son, Joseph's destiny began with a God dream for him. He later fulfilled his dream when God gave Pharaoh a dream that needed Joseph's help interpreting.

Genesis 41:14-16 shows the full circle in Joseph's life, "So Pharaoh sent for Joseph, and he was quickly brought from the dungeon. When he had shaved and changed his clothes, he came before Pharaoh. Pharaoh said to Joseph, 'I had a dream, and no one can interpret it. But I have heard it said of you that when you hear a dream you can interpret it.' 'I cannot do it,' Joseph replied to Pharaoh, 'but God will give Pharaoh the answer he desires.'

Joseph went on to interpret Pharaoh's dream, which was a strategy to save Egypt and the surrounding areas from a coming famine and in the course of it, Joseph was promoted to second in command in all of the land to oversee the implementation of the strategy.

Dreams are not just for special people; God promises that His Spirit is for all in Acts 2:17, "And it shall come to pass in the last days, says God, that I will pour out my Spirit on all people. Your sons and daughters will prophesy, your young men will see visions, your old men will dream dreams."

God anticipates communicating with mankind through dreams. He expects His children to learn to understand what He's communicating. It's part of life in the Spirit. Dreams are meant to be interpreted with the help of Holy Spirit, in relationship. God has given downloads of symbols and dream dictionaries to help us as we partner with Holy Spirit. If we rely only on the dictionaries, He'll change it up. It's not a formula; it's relationship and meant to bring us deeper. That being said, we're also expected to use the resources He's provided to grow in our understanding of how the Lord speaks.

If you're prophetic, you'll dream all night long, not just in the REM sleep cycle. You won't remember all of the dreams, nor are they all meaningful. As you're faithful to steward your dreams, they'll increase. God rewards faithfulness and sacrifice. Don't expect to remember your dreams or all of the important details without writing them down immediately. Details fade. It is a sacrifice to get up and write them down or record them on a voice recorder. It's supposed to be. That's your part; God won't do it for you.

I have seasons where I have significant dreams a lot, and others where my night season is quieter. So far, I range between 1-2 dreams I write down per month to 8-15 per month. As I've matured, I've learned which dreams are significant. Dreams that are important tend to become more clear as time goes by, like seeing a good movie. I may wake up, write it down and wonder what a dream was about. By the end of the day, it will stick with me and because it gets more vivid in my memory, I'll know to press into it. Other dreams are obviously prophetic upon waking and writing them down.

The vast majority of your dreams (~95%) will be about you. They'll become more about other people as you mature and if you have a strong intercessory gift. Also, as you increase in intimacy with God, you'll receive more dreams for others and get prophetic words at night for others.

John Paul Jackson talks about a clarity/cost principle. Dreams are symbolic and have a lower cost to accomplish. Their meanings or clarity are hidden and don't require a lot of effort on our part for them to come to pass. Visions that people see while they're sleeping look like dreams, except they are literal in meaning. Because there is a high clarity, there is also a high cost to accomplish. There is a process and a battle and the person needs to know that God said it and needs to hold onto the promise from God. The angel appearing to Jesus' father Joseph in a dream was a literal vision and required absolute obedience and confidence in the direction it gave.

Proverbs 25:2 instructs, "It's the glory of God to conceal a matter, but the glory of kings to search out a matter." God hides things for us, not from us. Dreams are a way for us to search out meaning and walk in our sonship with the King. Our approach to dream interpretation needs to reflect this principle.

Warning dreams are bigger/more dramatic so that people will take action to avoid the consequences. God gets our attention to prompt us into action and repentance. One of my daughters was struggling with rebellion when she was younger. I told her I was discerning her attitude was partnering with a demonic spirit of rebellion and I asked her if she wanted to repent. She said no. That night she had a dream where sharks were chasing her all over the pool trying to bite her and she couldn't get away from them. She was pretty scared because of the drama of the dream. She came to me with the dream and asked me to look up sharks in my dream dictionary. We looked it up and saw that sharks represent a spirit of rebellion. God got her attention and she repented then.

All revelation comes by Holy Spirit. We're not guaranteed an interpretation. God intentionally makes us uncomfortable so that we will seek out solutions and to draw us closer to Him. God doesn't just do this with believers, but with all people. There are examples in Scripture of kings having dreams where they were uncomfortable enough to seek answers. Joseph and Daniel were both called into kings to interpret dreams and bring revelation.

One of the biggest reasons people get stuck interpreting dreams is they get confused by something in a dream that doesn't make sense rationally. For example, they will be in a house that they know is theirs, yet the house has six kitchens instead of one. I dreamed about a previous church where I saw seventy people at their 2nd service instead of the thousands who normally attend. It didn't make sense in the dream. Just as I would react with surprise if I saw that in a movie, my soul observed the dream and was surprised, as well as my spirit. I personally cannot trust the emotions I have in a dream because it is my soul processing and doesn't mean it is part of the interpretation. If I had trusted the surprise I felt, I may have thought that the church was dying. Instead, I asked the Lord for the interpretation and He told me that they were moving into a season of equipping people and sending them out for ministry and that they were starting a ministry school. The number 70 in my dream symbolized when Jesus sent out 70 disciples to do ministry. I asked Him timing to know if it was a now word. I knew it was a prophetic word for them. I emailed my former pastors with the word that it was time to start a ministry school. They emailed me back and said a school was in the works and they hadn't told anybody yet. It was sweet confirmation to them that they were in the will and timing of the Lord.

INTERPRETATION PROCESS

I ask the Lord a series of six questions to arrive at an interpretation and application.

<u>Question 1</u>

First question I ask is, is this a spirit interaction, a literal vision, a symbolic dream, or a combination?

Is this a spirit interaction dream? A spirit interaction dream means it is literal and it actually happens during the night where a person's spirit travels at the Holy Spirit's leading to minister to someone. Depending upon the spiritual sensitivity of the people involved, they both may be aware of the interaction or just the one who saw the interaction in dream form. There may be symbolic components to the interaction, but the interaction literally happened. After a spirit interaction, the person will wake up and feel like the dream was real and really happened. We never attempt to "travel" in our dreams. This is strictly the Holy Spirit's prerogative and leading. When you have a spirit interaction dream with a prophet, you can consider what you received to be an impartation and/or a prophetic word. It is as valuable as if they stood before you during a meeting and delivered a word to you. I've had a number of spirit interaction dreams where I've received emotional, spiritual, and physical healing in the dreams. It's a very efficient way for God to meet our needs.

Is this a literal vision? A literal vision can be in pictorial form or can also be the voice of

God speaking during the night. God often releases literal direction during the night. When we moved into our townhouse in Raleigh, He spoke to me during the night not to decorate it because we wouldn't live there long.

Is this a symbolic dream that needs to be interpreted? An example of a symbolic dream is the one I had about my former pastors starting a ministry school.

Is this a combination of the above elements? I've had spirit interaction dreams twice where a prophet has bought me a new purse. This prophet carries a strong intercessory anointing, so I knew I had received an intercession impartation. There were other elements to the dream that were symbolic in nature, that needed interpreting.

Question 2

What kind of dream is this? I've grouped dreams into 12 categories:

1. Healing- emotional, physical, spiritual healing is released through the dream. Wake up healed and feeling better.
2. Directional- God gives direction, specific calling, identity, and releases the courage to accomplish His will.
3. Flushing- This dream cleanses you of spiritual or emotional trauma you were exposed to throughout your week. If you were around a demonic spirit of lust, you may have a sexual dream with lust in it for the purpose of the demonic not attaching to you. These kinds of flushing dreams can be a little uncomfortable because of their nature. If you're not in bondage to sexual sin, you can be assured that the dream is just cleansing you. I don't write flushing dreams in my journal.
4. Deliverance- torment healed and released from you by the Lord. After a particularly difficult season, in the course of a month, I had five dreams where our church's deliverance and inner healing pastor was ministering to me. After the month of deliverance dreams, I was fairly well healed and recovered from the season.
5. Self-condition- This type of dream shows you what you look like in the spirit and where you are overall. Often, this type of dream comes through you seeing what

your house looks like in a dream. You know it's your house but it doesn't look like the physical one you live in. If the foundation is faulty and the roof leaks, those are clues that you need a new foundation in the Lord and a better spiritual covering. If the floor is new but needs sweeping, that shows you that your foundation is good but needs some clean up. Pay attention to the details and pray that the Lord would fix what you can see needs help in the dream. At some point you'll have another house dream and you'll see the progress you've made.

6. Word of Knowledge/Invention/Business Plans/Prophetic- These types of dreams give you strategies directly from Heaven. The world's best-selling bow and arrow set was designed through the blueprint being released from God in this type of dream. These dreams solve problems. I had one of these dreams once where I believe God was alerting me to what these feel like, yet it was a practice run. In the dream, I saw a graph and saw that the mathematical number Pi (3.14159...) was equal to 90 degrees on the graph. This doesn't make sense in the mathematical world, but the next time, I've been prepared to receive the blueprint from God.

7. Soul processing/Emotions- These are dreams where your soul plays out scenarios for the sake of not getting stuck or wounded in relationships. They are not prophetic in nature. I don't write soul dreams down in my journal.

8. Seer/Spiritual Structures/Revelatory Concepts - These are dreams where God shows you how things function or look in the spiritual realm. I had a dream one night where I was sexual with a man I had just met. I woke up feeling unclean and wondered if it was a flushing dream. Then the Lord spoke to me and said, "Intimacy does not exist without a process." He showed me that in the world today where people share so many details of their lives on social media, people feel like they know each other. Yet, they still feel empty in relationships, because the knowledge doesn't translate to intimacy without the process of sharing covenant life together.

9. Intercession – This is a dream where you see something about yourself or others that needs to be prayed through. Whether it's an enemy plan or how things just are, the intercession approach is the same. Cancel any assignments against the person and release the plan of God in his/her life.

10. Spiritual Warfare – This is an intercession dream or series of dreams where your spirit is praying actively in the dream. You may see snakes or bad guys or witches or other things chasing you. As your spirit gets stronger, you'll defeat these enemy forces in the dream. If the dream ends with you cutting off the snake's head or killing the witch, it is accomplished in the spirit and no further action needs to be taken. If you awake before you finish off the enemy, you'll need to pray through it. God will confirm to you when you've been successful. Remember, we don't war against flesh and blood. We war against the demonic.

11. Flying – Hands down my favorite kind of dream. These mean you're flying above a situation or that you've gained spiritual authority and finesse. Your spirit will awake refreshed and energized.

12. Impartation – These come with the spirit interaction dreams where someone imparts to you something that prior to the dream you couldn't do at that level. Be faithful to steward the increase in your life.

Question 3

Who is this dream about?

1. If you're the main character in the dream, it's about you.
2. If you're in it, but the dream can go on without you, it's about others in the dream and your role is usually intercession.
3. If you're observing, it's about others with little impact on you.

Question 4

What is the overall theme?

Identify the overall theme. That is important to the overall interpretation.

Question 5

What is the timing of the dream?

Does this dream relate to the past, present or future? Identifying timing will help you with application.

Question 6

What is the appropriate response?

How are you to respond to having this dream? How do you steward it?

1. Intercession?
2. Tell the person? If telling the person can potentially create fear, don't share it, just pray through it.
3. Dialogue with God?
4. Direction change?

There are some common dreams that people have and wonder what the interpretation is. Anything that is negative is to get your attention to pray through it and make any necessary adjustments. I'll list them here:

1. Flying – Flying above situations. Spiritual advancement is coming.
2. Vehicles – Your ministry or vocation. The bigger the vehicle or plane or boat, the bigger the audience and responsibility.
3. Houses – What you look like in your personal situation.
4. Hallways/Stairs/Hotels/Elevators/Escalators – Transition. Pay attention to the direction. Up is always good. Going down to a basement can mean foundation work.
5. Falling – Situation in life is out of control.
6. Loose Teeth/Teeth Missing or Falling Out – Lacking wisdom, or relationships need adjusting.
7. Can't Push Gas Pedal/Arm Can't Throw Ball/Can't Run – Something is not fully operating in your life.
8. Can't Speak or Yell – Warning that you're not praying or declaring enough.

9. Can't Unlock School Locker/Can't Find Class Schedule/Miss Exam – Something is trying to stop you from what you need to learn.

10. Going to the Bathroom/Showering – Deliverance is happening. If going in public, deliverance will be public. Embrace it for necessary freedom.

11. Naked – God is helping you to be transparent and authentic.

12. School/Exam – Training for next level of proficiency.

13. Money/Checks – Favor, Finances coming to you if receiving money in dream. Loss of favor, finances if losing money in dream.

14. You're a Child in Dream – God's going to help you grow up, some growth was stunted.

15. 2 Dreams Back to Back/2 Scenes in Same Dream – different perspective of same issue.

16. Can't See Face of Person – often is Holy Spirit

17. Don't Know Person but Can See Face – an angel or someone you may meet.

PRAYER ACTIVATION

Commit to stewarding your dreams. Ask the Lord for more revelation and practice interpreting. In the space provided, write out a dream you've had, then use the principles here to interpret your dream. Dialogue with the Lord for further understanding.

_____

_____

_____

_____

_____

_____

_____

_____

_____

_____

_____

_____

_____

_____

_____

_____

_____

_____

_____

_____

Annie Blouin

CHAPTER 12

PROPHETIC PROTOCOL

WEIGHING, JUDGING, STEWARDING PROPHETIC WORDS

When you receive a prophetic word, it is your job to immediately witness to the word or not with your spirit, not with your soul, mind, will, emotions, or unbelief. Words from Heaven carry peace, joy, and a knowing. God wrote all of our days before He ever created us and downloaded that into our spirits before we were born. When we receive a prophetic word, our spirit recognizes it and it helps our mind be aware of whom we are.

If you witness that the word is accurate, respond with faith and say yes to God; no matter what it takes, no matter the process. Dialogue with Him about it. Believe wholeheartedly. Recognize that most likely there will be a process to prepare you for it. Timing. Timing. Timing. Timing is everything, don't run ahead of your season or try to short circuit the preparation process. Ask God what your part is. Do not take an attitude of "I'll just put this on the shelf and see what happens". That is not faith and isn't co-laboring with God. As you're walking with God, words that you agreed with God about may spring up suddenly and surprise you with their fulfillment. It is the fact that you said yes in your heart and pursued God and your current assignment that allowed them to come to fruition. Other words will take more sowing on your part to bring to harvest. Review your prophetic words often and keep them in front of you. Wage war with your prophetic words by declaring them out loud. Your destiny and identity is at stake. Be faithful to prepare yourself through school and study. You can't be a doctor to fulfill a prophetic destiny if you don't graduate from medical school. Most of all: Believe.

PRAYER ACTIVATION

Ask the Lord if there are any prophetic words that He had for you that you didn't witness correctly to or didn't steward correctly and therefore, missed. Journal here anything He shows you about partnering with Him to fulfill your destiny.

_____

_____

_____

_____

_____

_____

_____

_____

_____

_____

_____

_____

_____

PROPHETIC PROTOCOL

Prophetic words are meant to honor people and show them how much God loves them. The DNA of the prophetic must be honor and love. I love to prophesy over people so that I can see them how the Father sees them. I grow in love for them much more after I see from the Father's perspective. I also love to listen to words over people, so that I can help them run their races well. The prophetic atmosphere is one of love, energy, and excitement. Merely being in the prophetic environment will stir your heart for love with Jesus and destiny.

PROPHETIC ACCOUNTABILITY

As prophetic people, we are accountable to show people love and respect. We have a duty to practice our gifting to prepare for increase. When we realize that we have delivered a word that isn't right, we need to take responsibility to apologize and clean up any mess we may have made. We are charged with getting our identity and value from being God's children and not from our gifting or leadership position. We are obligated to grow in character and grow in our intimacy with God.

Prophetic people need to be open to correction and under authority of our pastors. Being submitted to authority is important for our spiritual protection and for our ability to serve. Prophetic people are prone to being picked off by the enemy if they are not in community with other believers and submitted to their church leadership. If this has been a place of wounding for you, pursue healing and ask God who healthy leaders are in your area that you can serve.

Different churches have different prophetic cultures. Some have prophetic teams available after services to pray for people, some allow words to be given during the service, some allow words to be given to the pastor leading the meeting. Find out what your church's prophetic culture is and don't judge how they steward the call of God on their lives in leading a church. God put them in place and has a mandate for them to follow. Pray for them to follow God well. As you grow in your character and prophetic gifting, God will open doors for you to serve.

PRAYER ACTIVATION

Dialogue with God about any areas of prophetic accountability you have questions about. Write any questions here to ask your church's prophetic leader later.

_____

_____

_____

_____

_____

_____

_____

_____

_____

_____

_____

_____

_____

_____

_____

_____

_____

PRAYER ACTIVATION

Journal any further thoughts or questions you have about your prophetic journey here.

_____

_____

_____

_____

_____

_____

_____

_____

_____

_____

_____

_____

_____

_____

_____

_____

_____

_____

Congratulations for studying and growing in your prophetic gifting! May the Lord bless you with joy and opportunities to share His heart with people as you go through life.

ABOUT ANNIE BLOUIN

Annie Blouin teaches Prophetic Revelation at Catch the Fire Raleigh's School of Revival. She has keen insight into the supernatural and equips her students to prophesy and operate supernaturally with a sound Biblical foundation. Her heart is to see Revivalists influence every area of society with love and wisdom. She has been happily married to Joe for 21 years and they have three beautiful children who love the Lord.

Made in the USA
Middletown, DE
31 March 2017